English for
Nursing

1

Vocational English
Course Book

Ros Wright and Bethany Cagnol

with Maria Spada Symonds
Series editor David Bonamy

Contents

Meeting colleagues

- introduce yourself to a hospital team
- read a nursing schedule
- meet patients and their visitors
- escort a patient for tests

Introducing yourself to the team

Listening **1** ▶ 🔘 **02** Look at this notice board. Then listen to three conversations. Who is speaking in each conversation? Write the number of the conversation (1–3) next to the job titles (a–e).

Ward C
Let's welcome the following new members to the team:

Ward Sister Margaret Jenkins

Staff Nurse Gillian Campbell

Student Nurse David Spencer

Charge Nurse Paul Gallagher

Healthcare Assistant Amy Bower

a) charge nurse ____, ____
b) ward sister ____
c) staff nurse ____
d) healthcare assistant ____
e) student nurse ____

Language

Present simple of *be*		
I am ('m)	I am not ('m not)	Am I?
you/we/they are ('re)	you/we/they are not (aren't)	Are you/we/they?
he/she/it is ('s)	he/she/it is not (isn't)	Is he/she/it?

We can use *be* to say a person's name, job and country.	*What's your name? I'm Staff Nurse Sophie Taylor.* *Are you Sister Butler? Yes, I am.* *Is she a student nurse? No, she isn't.* *He's a student nurse.* *They're healthcare assistants.* *I'm not from Turkey. I'm from Syria.*

2 Complete these conversations with the correct form of *be*.

1   Mike: Hello, I (1) _____ Staff Nurse Mike Davies.
(2) _____ you the charge nurse?
Sonya: Hi. Yes, I (3) _____ . I'm Sonya Chaudhry.
Mike: Nice to meet you, Sonya. Where are you from?
Sonya: I'm from India.

2   Student nurse: Excuse me, (4) _____ you Ward Sister Kennedy?
Sister: No, I (5) _____ not.
Student nurse: Oh! Sorry about that. (6) _____ she in Ward C?
Sister: No, she (7) _____ . She (8) _____ in Ward B.
Student nurse: Oh, OK. Thanks very much.

3   Student nurse: Excuse me, I need a healthcare assistant.
Healthcare assistant: I (9) _____ a healthcare assistant. Can I help you?
Student nurse: Hi, sorry. I (10) _____ a student nurse. I need a little help.
Healthcare assistant: No problem. What do you need?

Speaking   **3**   Work in pairs. Introduce yourselves. Use this model to help you.

A: Hi. My name's [your name]. I'm a[n] [your job title].
B: Hello, [partner's name]. I'm [your name], a[n] [your job title].
A: Hi, really nice to meet you. Are you from [partner's country]?
B: Yes, I am! And you? Where are you from?
A: I'm from [your country].
B: Nice to meet you, too!

Language

Present simple

I/you/we/they live	I/you/we/they do not (don't) live	Do I/you/we/they live?
he/she/it lives	he/she/it does not (doesn't) live	Does he/she/it live?

We use the **present simple** to talk about something that is always or usually true.	They **work** in this hospital.
We also use it to talk about things that happen regularly.	He **walks** to the hospital every day.

---

4 Complete this text with the correct present simple form of the verbs in brackets.

Dale is an agency nurse from the Nurse Pro Agency.
He is a Canadian but he (1) _____ (not live) in Canada.
He (2) _____ (live) in the UK now and he (3) _____ (work) here too. Dale (4) _____ (have) two friends at this hospital: Peter and Marcus; but he (5) _____ (not work) the same shifts as them. 'I (6) _____ (have) classes during the day,' he says, 'and so I usually (7) _____ (work) during the night shift.'

Reading a nursing schedule

Telling the time

Nurses use the **twelve-hour clock** when they talk to patients, visitors and colleagues.	12.00: twelve o'clock 3 p.m.
We often use the **24-hour clock** for schedules, documents and charts.	14.00: two o'clock/fourteen hundred hours 8.20: eight twenty/twenty past eight

Prepositions of time

We use *at* with clock times.	I start/finish work/my shift *at* 7 a.m.
We use *in* with parts of the day and longer periods of time.	*in* the morning/afternoon/evening but: *at* night

Vocabulary **1** Label illustrations A–H with the times in the box.

> 20.00   12.00   14.45   23.30   8.15 a.m.   9.20 a.m.   24.00   3 p.m.

2 Match these ways of telling the time (1–8) to the times in the box in 1.

1 nine twenty in the morning _____
2 eight o'clock in the evening _____
3 midday _____
4 quarter to three in the afternoon _____
5 half past eleven at night _____
6 three in the afternoon _____
7 quarter past eight in the morning _____
8 midnight _____

Speaking **3** Work in pairs. Ask and answer these questions with your partner.

1 What time is it now?
2 What time do you get up in the morning?
3 What time do you start work/your shift every day?
4 What time do you/does your shift finish?

A: What time is it now?
B: It's half past seven.

Listening 4 🔊 03 Listen to Tyler, an agency nurse, checking his schedule with Karen, who works at the Nurse Pro Agency. Complete Tyler's time sheet.

Nurse Pro Agency
Employee time sheet

Name: Tyler Baker **Week N° 33**

Day	Clock in	Clock out
Monday		
Tuesday		
Wednesday		
Thursday		
Friday		
Saturday		
Sunday		

Speaking 5 Student A, look at the information on this page. Student B, look at the information on page 68. Follow the instructions.

Student A

Look at this hospital facilities schedule. Take the role of patient or visitor and ask Student B questions to complete the information.

	Midland Town Hospital Hospital facilities
Visiting hours	2.00 p.m. – 4.00 p.m. daily 6.30 p.m. – 8.00 p.m. daily
Car park	Monday to Friday: _____
Bank	Weekdays: _____
Restaurant	Monday to Friday: _____ Saturday and Sunday: 10.00 a.m. – 5.00 p.m
Coffee shop	Monday to Friday: _____ Saturday and Sunday: 12.00 noon – 6.30 p.m.
Gift shop	Monday, Wednesday, Thursday: 10.00 a.m. – 8.00 p.m. Tuesday and Friday: _____ Saturday and Sunday: 10.00 a.m. – 5.00 p.m.
Newsstand	Monday to Friday: 10.00 a.m. – 8.00 p.m. Saturday and Sunday: _____
Patient mealtimes	Breakfast: _____ Dinner: 12.30 p.m. Tea: _____ Beverages: 10.00 a.m. and 7.15 p.m.

What are the visiting hours?
What are the opening hours of the bank?
What time does the car park open/close?
When is breakfast?

Meeting patients and their visitors

1 ▶ 04 Listen to four nurses meeting their patients for the first time and tick ✓ the correct patient name for each nurse.

Patient list (Rooms 11–14)				
Staff nurse	Susie Arnold	Mrs Coxen	Kendra	Mr Williams
Anja				
Katya				
Max				
Denny				

2 Listen again and complete these expressions.

1 ☐ _____ I come _____ ?
2 ☐ Yes, of _____ .
3 ☐ It's Mrs Coxen, _____ it?
4 ☐ I'm taking _____ of you.
5 ☐ Please _____ me Susie.
6 ☐ _____ to disturb you.
7 ☐ I'm looking _____ you.
8 ☐ How _____ you today?

3 ▶ 05 Listen again to Denny and tick ✓ the expressions in 2 that he uses.

Vocabulary **4** Complete this family tree with the underlined words in the box. Then complete sentences a–e with the rest of the words in the box.

> aunt   brother   cousin (x2)   father   father-in-law   granddaughter   grandfather
> grandmother   grandson   husband   mother   mother-in-law   sister   son   wife

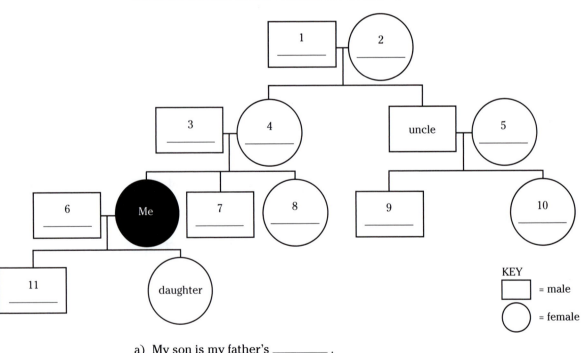

KEY
☐ = male
◯ = female

a) My son is my father's _____ .
b) I am my husband's _____ .
c) My daughter is my mother's _____ .
d) My husband's mother is my _____ .
e) My father is my husband's _____ .

Speaking **5** Draw a picture of a family and label the people with words from 4. Then work in pairs. Look at the information on page 68. Follow the instructions.

6 Work in small groups. Look at this illustration of a hospital ward. Put a tick ✓ if you think the visitors are doing the right thing and a cross ✗ if you think they are doing the wrong thing.

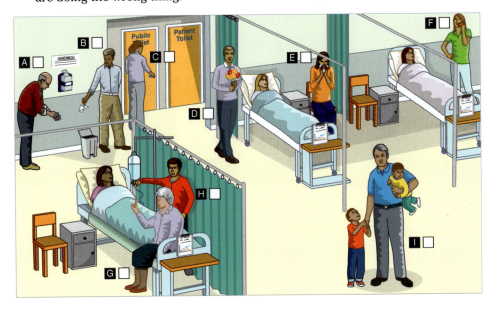

7 Read this hospital guide and check your answers in 6.

Visitor's code

Please do not
- touch wounds, drips, catheters or medical equipment.
- visit more than two at a time.
- use the patients' toilets.
- bring flowers onto the wards.
- visit the hospital if you are suffering from a bad cold, flu, diarrhoea and/or vomiting.
- drop litter.
- bring children under 12 to visit (unless agreed in advance).

Please do
- visit between 2.30 p.m. and 8.30 p.m.
- turn off your mobile phone on the wards.
- wash your hands when you enter and leave the ward.
- extinguish all cigarettes before you arrive at the hospital.
- use the chairs provided.
- speak to the ward sister if there is a problem.

GH

Speaking **8** Work in small groups. Answer these questions.

In your country or place of work …
1 What are the visiting hours?
2 How many people can visit a patient at one time?
3 Can a parent or guardian stay overnight with their child?
4 Can brothers and sisters visit each other?

9 Work in pairs. Practise politely asking the visitors in 6 not to do something.

Excuse me, please don't sit on the patient's bed.
I'm sorry, you can't sit on the patient's bed.

Escorting a patient for tests

1 Work in pairs. Look at these photos of medical equipment and complete the labels with the letters in the box.

> CT ECG MRI X

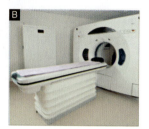

_____ -ray machine   _____ scanner   _____ scanner   _____ machine

Pronunciation **2** 🔊 06 Listen to the names of the medical equipment in 1 and repeat.

Language

Ordinal numbers

1st first	6th sixth	11th eleventh	22nd twenty-second
2nd second	7th seventh	12th twelfth	23rd twenty-third
3rd third	8th eighth	13th thirteenth	31st thirty-first
4th fourth	9th ninth	20th twentieth	
5th fifth	10th tenth	21st twenty-first	

We use **ordinal numbers** for dates.	6th July 1975 23rd October 2001
We say dates like this:	4th August 1914: the **fourth** of August, nineteen fourteen 31st March 2011: the **thirty-first** of March, two thousand and eleven
But we often write dates like this on forms: day.month.year	06.07.1975

Listening **3** 🔊 07 Listen to a nurse taking patients to the Radiology Department and write the correct test for each patient in a–c on this appointments sheet.

> ## Radiology Dept.
> **Appointments**   **Date:** 20.11.20____
>
> | 13:30 | (1) Amira _____ | 14.30 | (3) Dorothy _____ | 15.30 | (5) Emilia _____ |
> |---|---|---|---|---|---|
> | DOB: | (2) _____ | DOB: | (4) _____ | DOB: | (6) _____ |
> | Test: | a) _____ | Test: | b) _____ | Test: | c) _____ |

4 Listen again and complete each patient's name and date of birth (DOB) in 1–6 on the appointments sheet in 3.

5 Work in pairs. Look at the audio script for track 07 on pages 72–73 and practise reading aloud the dates of birth. Then dictate three dates of birth for your partner to write down.

Vocabulary **6** Label the illustration with the words in the box.

> blanket   trolley   walking stick   wheelchair

7 Put the words in 1–5 in the correct order to make sentences and questions.

1 now / it's / for your X-ray / time
2 ready / are / you / ?
3 your identity bracelet / can I just see / first / , please / ?
4 full name / your / what's / ?
5 on your bracelet / can I swipe / , please / the code / ?

Listening **8** ▶ 🔊 **08** Listen to the first part of a conversation between Kelly, a staff nurse, and Jake, a patient she is escorting to the Radiology Department, and check your answers in 7.

9 ▶ 🔊 **09** Listen to the second part of the conversation between Kelly and Jake and choose the correct words in *italics*.

1 Jake uses a *walking stick / wheelchair / trolley* to go to Radiology.
2 He feels *cold / tired / weak*. (2 answers)
3 The nurse gives him a *book / bracelet / blanket*.
4 The Radiology nurse is called *Claire / Katie / Sally*.
5 Jake's appointment is at *10.00 / 10.30 / 11.30*.

10 Kelly uses certain expressions to check that her patient is feeling comfortable. Complete these expressions with the words in the box. Then listen again and check your answers.

> better   help   let   warm

1 Let me _____ you.
2 Are you _____ enough?
3 _____ me give you a blanket.
4 Is that _____?

Speaking **11** Work in small groups. Look at the audio script for tracks 08 and 09 on page 73 and practise the conversations. Then swap roles and repeat the activity.

12 Work in pairs. Practise escorting a patient to the Radiology Department. Follow these steps.

- Introduce yourself to the patient.
- Tell the patient it is time for their test.
- Check the patient's identity bracelet.
- Ask the patient how they want to go to the Radiology Department.
- Make sure your patient is comfortable.
- Introduce the patient to the radiology nurse.

Then ask another pair to listen and check that you have followed all the steps. Swap roles and repeat the activity.

2

Nursing assessment

- check patient details
- describe symptoms
- assess common childhood diseases
- take a blood sample

Checking patient details

Reading **1** Read these patient details and answer the questions.

> GP (general practitioner) = family doctor

Birmingham General Hospital

Patient details

Title: Mr.   First name(s): Kyle   Surname: McDonald

Gender: ☒ M ☐ F   Marital status: single

DOB: 12.09.1982   Occupation: construction worker

Address: 5 Davis Close, Nottingham NG1 9QB

Tel: (mobile) 4779 003 5491   Email: kmcdonald@telepo.co.uk

GP: Dr Tanya Millet

Next of kin: Suzanne McDonald   Relationship to patient: mother

1 Is the patient a man or a woman?
2 When is the patient's birthday?
3 What is the patient's job?
4 Is the patient married?
5 Who is the patient's family doctor?
6 Who is Suzanne McDonald?

Listening **2** ▶ 🔊 10 Listen to two conversations and tick ✓ the information the person asks for.

1 The adviser asks for the patient's
☐ name and surname.
☐ date of birth.
☐ address.
☐ telephone number.
☐ email address.
☐ next of kin.

2 The nurse asks for the patient's
☐ name and surname.
☐ date of birth.
☐ address.
☐ telephone number.
☐ email address.
☐ marital status.

3 Listen again and complete these tables.

1

Patient name	James (1) _____
Next of kin	(2) _____
Telephone number	(3) _____

2

Patient name	Amir (4) _____
DOB	(5) _____
Address	(6) 81 Avenue Mahmoud _____
Email	(7) _____@teleco.com

Language

4 Work in pairs. Complete these questions with *what*, *where* or *who*. Then practise asking and answering the questions.

1 _____'s your surname/first name/full name?
2 _____ do you live?
3 _____'s your address/email address/mobile phone number?
4 _____'s your date of birth?
5 _____'s your GP?
6 _____'s your next of kin?
7 _____'s his/her relationship to you?

Speaking

5 Work in pairs. Think of names that will help you understand letters that are difficult for you. Then practise checking the spelling.

A: Is that B as in Bob or D as in Diane?
B: It's B for Bob.

Nurses can use names to check letters that are difficult to understand on the phone.
B for *Bob*
P as in *Peter*

6 Work in pairs. Student A, look at the information on this page. Student B, look at the information on page 69. Follow the instructions.

Student A

1 You are a patient and this is your patient record. Answer Student B's questions.

Patient details   **GH**

Name:	Gregorz Rogalewicz
Gender:	male
DOB:	25.07.1979
Country of origin:	Poland
Telephone number:	011-48-555-293-078
GP:	Jaroslaw Galucka
Email:	greg.rogalewicz@oliwa.com
Address:	ul. Lewakowskiego 36/39 Skr. poczt. 54
Next of kin:	Anja Rogalewicz
Relationship to patient:	mother

2 Swap roles. You are the nurse and Student B is a patient. Ask Student B questions to complete this patient record.

Patient details   **GH**

Name:	_____
Gender:	female
DOB:	_____
Country of origin:	_____
Telephone number:	_____
GP:	_____
Email:	_____
Address:	_____
Next of kin:	_____
Relationship to patient:	_____

Describing symptoms

1 Match illustrations A–N to symptoms 1–14.

1 cough	8 runny nose
2 dizzy	9 skin rash
3 earache	10 sore throat
4 fever	11 stomachache
5 headache	12 sweaty
6 itchy	13 swollen glands
7 nauseous	14 tired

Pronunciation **2** ▶ 🔊 **11** Listen and check your answers in 1. Then listen again and repeat.

Speaking **3** Work in small groups. What do you think are the top five reasons for visiting a GP in the UK? Put the symptoms in the correct order (1–5), beginning with the most common. Then check the answers at the bottom of the page.

4 What do you think are the top five reasons for visiting a GP in your country? Discuss.

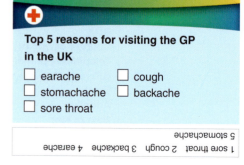

Top 5 reasons for visiting the GP in the UK

☐ earache   ☐ cough
☐ stomachache   ☐ backache
☐ sore throat

1 sore throat 2 cough 3 backache 4 earache
5 stomachache

Language

Talking about symptoms		
	Describing symptoms	**Asking about symptoms**
be + adjective	*I'm tired.*	*Is he nauseous ?*
feel + adjective	*She feels dizzy.*	*Does it feel itchy?*
have + (adjective +) noun	*He has a sore throat.*	*Does he have a sore throat?*

5 Work in pairs. Look at the symptoms in 1 and write adjective (*A*), noun (*N*), or adjective + noun (*A+N*) next to each one.

6 Match 1–5 to a–e to make questions.

1 Do you   a) feel today?
2 How do you   b) have a runny nose?
3 Do you have any   c) your symptoms?
4 What are   d) other symptoms?
5 Do you have a   e) temperature?

7 An anxious father calls the doctor's surgery and speaks to the practice nurse. Read the answers he gave about his son. Write the nurse's questions.

1 A: _____?   B: My son's name is Saul Chambers.
2 A: _____?   B: He's three.
3 A: _____?   B: He has a bad stomachache.
4 A: _____?   B: Yes, it's 37.5°.
5 A: _____?   B: No other symptoms, no.

Speaking   **8** Work in pairs. Student A, look at the information on this page. Student B, look at the information on page 69. Follow the instructions.

Student A

1 You are ill and these are your symptoms.
You
- have a skin rash.
- have a headache.
- are sweaty.
- have a slight fever (38°C/100°F).

Answer Student B's questions, explaining your symptoms. Student B will give you a possible diagnosis.

2 Swap roles. Ask Student B about his/her symptoms and tick ✓ the symptoms he/she has.

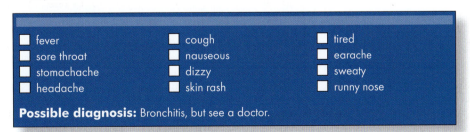

☐ fever   ☐ cough   ☐ tired
☐ sore throat   ☐ nauseous   ☐ earache
☐ stomachache   ☐ dizzy   ☐ sweaty
☐ headache   ☐ skin rash   ☐ runny nose

Possible diagnosis: Bronchitis, but see a doctor.

Hello, how do you feel today? Do you have a temperature? Do you have a sore throat?

Assessing common childhood diseases

Vocabulary **1** Work in small groups. Match photos A–C to the childhood diseases 1–3.

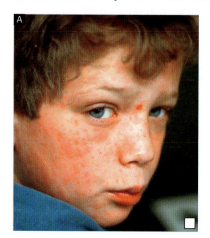 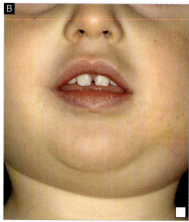 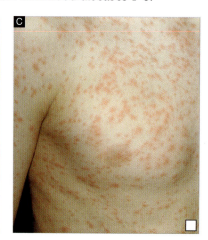

1 rubella   2 measles   3 mumps

2 Work in pairs. Match the symptoms in the box to the childhood diseases in 1. Write *1* for *rubella*, *2* for *measles* or *3* for *mumps* above each word. Some symptoms can appear in more than one disease.

> cough   fever   headache   nausea   rash   runny nose   sore throat   swollen glands

Reading **3** Read this patient education leaflet and check your answers in 2.

MMR information leaflet

What is MMR?
The MMR vaccine protects your child against these highly infectious childhood diseases: measles, mumps and rubella.

What are the symptoms?
- measles: cough, fever, rash, runny nose and sore throat
- mumps: fever, headache, nausea and swollen glands
- rubella: fever, headache, rash (red-pink colour), runny nose, sore throat and swollen glands

When to give the vaccine
- When your baby is 13 months old, make an appointment with your family doctor or public health nurse for the first MMR vaccine.
- At 4–5 years your child will receive the second vaccine (or booster) at school.
- → The vaccines are free of charge.

What happens after the vaccination?
Does your child have a fever? Is the injection area sore, swollen or red? If yes, give your child paracetamol or ibuprofen.

---

4 Work in pairs. Read the leaflet in 3 again and answer these questions.
1 Who is this leaflet for?
2 What do the letters MMR stand for?
3 How old are children when they receive the MMR vaccine? (2 answers)
4 Some children have symptoms after the vaccine. What are they?
5 How much does the MMR vaccine cost?
6 What is the treatment for these symptoms?

5   `▶ ⏱ 12`   Listen to three conversations and tick ✓ each patient's symptoms.

	Cough	Fever	Headache	Nausea	Rash	Runny nose	Sore throat	Swollen glands
Chelsea								
Milly								
Isabelle								

6   Work in pairs. Make a diagnosis of Chelsea, Milly and Isabelle.

Language

Adverbs of frequency

We use **adverbs of frequency** with the present simple to say how often we do things.

never   *sometimes*   *often*   *usually*   *always*

0% ————————————————→ 100%

Adverbs of frequency go before the main verb.	Patients with mumps **don't usually have** a rash.
Adverbs of frequency go after the verb *be*.	*I'm often* very tired after work.

---

7   Rewrite these sentences with the adverb of frequency in the correct position.

Children receive their second MMR vaccine at school. (usually)
Children usually receive their second MMR vaccine at school.

1   My son is feverish after a vaccine. (often)
2   Most people catch childhood diseases more than once. (never)
3   Babies have symptoms after the MMR vaccine. (sometimes)
4   Patients with measles are not infectious after the rash appears. (usually)

Writing   **8**   Complete this extract from a leaflet about chickenpox with the words in the box.

> childhood disease   hot   infectious   itchy   rash   rest   stop   symptom

> Chickenpox, or varicella (medical term), is another common (1) _____ .
> The first (2) _____ is usually a(n) (3) _____ all over the body, which is
> red and (4) _____ . It appears during the first 24 hours. Children often feel very
> (5) _____ and have a temperature of about 38°C. The best treatment for
> chickenpox is (6) _____ . You can use calamine lotion to (7) _____ the itching.
> Children with chickenpox are (8) _____ for a few days before the rash appears.

9   Complete this extract from a leaflet about scarlet fever with the expressions in
the box. Choose the correct words in *italics*.

> a common *childhood / children* disease   *has / have* a fever, a sore throat
> *is / are* infectious for three   school for five *day / days*
> treatment *for / to* scarlet fever   under *their / your* arm

> Scarlet fever, or scarletina (medical term), is still (1) _____ in the developing
> world. Children who catch this disease (2) _____ and a pink tongue.
> They also get a rash which is usually (3) _____ or in the groin. Children
> (4) _____ to eight days before symptoms appear. The only (5) _____
> is antibiotics. Children should not go to (6) _____ after they begin treatment.

Taking a blood sample

Vocabulary **1** Work in pairs. Match 1–7 in the illustrations to words a–g.

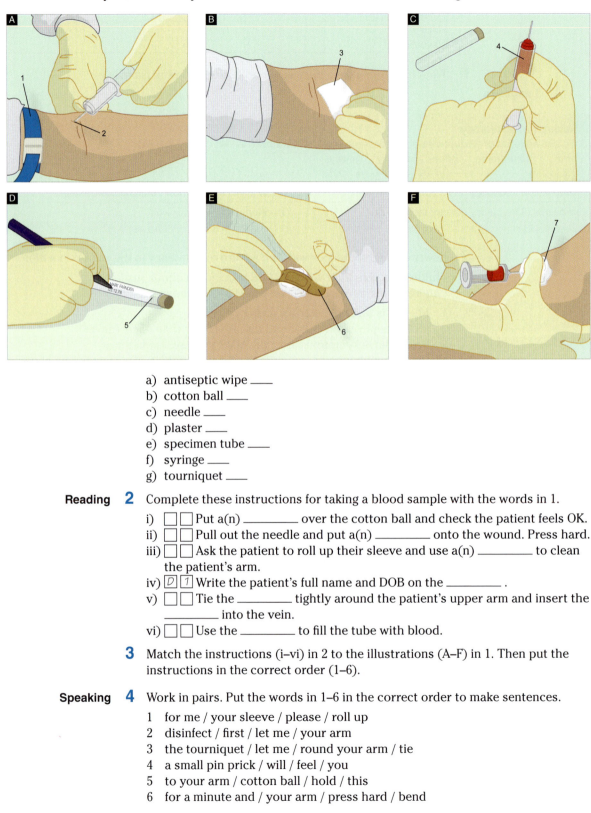

a) antiseptic wipe _____
b) cotton ball _____
c) needle _____
d) plaster _____
e) specimen tube _____
f) syringe _____
g) tourniquet _____

Reading **2** Complete these instructions for taking a blood sample with the words in 1.

i) ☐☐ Put a(n) _____ over the cotton ball and check the patient feels OK.
ii) ☐☐ Pull out the needle and put a(n) _____ onto the wound. Press hard.
iii) ☐☐ Ask the patient to roll up their sleeve and use a(n) _____ to clean the patient's arm.
iv) ☑D ☑1 Write the patient's full name and DOB on the _____ .
v) ☐☐ Tie the _____ tightly around the patient's upper arm and insert the _____ into the vein.
vi) ☐☐ Use the _____ to fill the tube with blood.

3 Match the instructions (i–vi) in 2 to the illustrations (A–F) in 1. Then put the instructions in the correct order (1–6).

Speaking **4** Work in pairs. Put the words in 1–6 in the correct order to make sentences.

1 for me / your sleeve / please / roll up
2 disinfect / first / let me / your arm
3 the tourniquet / let me / round your arm / tie
4 a small pin prick / will / feel / you
5 to your arm / cotton ball / hold / this
6 for a minute and / your arm / press hard / bend

Listening **5** ▶ 🎧 13 Listen to a nurse taking a blood sample and check your answers in 4.

6 Listen again and choose the correct words in *italics*.
1 Alessandro doesn't like *needles / blood / pain*.
2 The nurse asks Alessandro to *read a book / look out of the window / drink some water*. Why?
3 Alessandro feels *cold / dizzy / tired*.
4 The nurse gives Alessandro *some juice / a cookie / a cup of coffee*. Why?

Speaking **7** Work in small groups. Answer questions 2 and 4 in 6.

8 Work in small groups. Brainstorm symptoms people may have during a blood test.

9 Work in pairs. Take turns talking to a patient to relax him/her while you take a blood sample.
Tell me about your job/your day/your grandchildren.

10 Roleplay taking a blood sample. Then swap roles and repeat the activity.
Student A
You are the nurse. You are taking a blood sample from Student B. Use the sentences in 4 to help you. Don't forget to talk to the patient to relax him/her.
Student B
You are the patient and you feel scared and dizzy.

Pronunciation **11** ▶ 🎧 14 Listen and complete these sentences.
1 If you feel _____, let me know. (Y / N)
2 If you feel _____, tell me. (Y / N)
3 If you feel _____, let me know. (Y / N)
4 If you feel _____, tell me. (Y / N)

12 Listen again. Does the nurse sound reassuring? Circle *yes* (Y) or *no* (N) in 11. Then listen again and repeat, paying attention to the intonation.

Speaking **13** Work in pairs. Student A, imagine you are one of the people in 1–4 below. Student B, you are a nurse. Use the pictures and expressions in this lesson to roleplay taking a blood sample. Then swap roles and repeat the activity.
1 Mrs Anita Naidu doesn't like blood and she sometimes feels dizzy. She has three grandchildren and she likes to talk about them – a lot.
2 Mr Eric Margolis doesn't like needles and he always feels nauseous when he gives blood. He's a taxi driver and he often meets famous actors. He plays golf.
3 Aisha is eight years old and she doesn't like needles. She's very good at maths but hates English. Her best friend is Jaq and they love playing Wii together.
4 Harry is 19, an economics student and part-time DJ on an online radio station, playing retro 80s music. He faints when he sees blood.

3

The patient ward

- monitor body temperature
- recognise rooms in a patient ward
- talk about nursing duties
- describe the qualities of a responsible nurse

Monitoring body temperature

Vocabulary

1 Work in small groups. Match photos A–D to words 1–4.

A

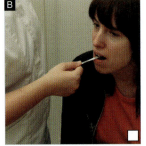
B

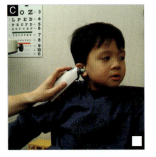
C

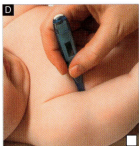
D

1 digital thermometer	3 oral thermometer
2 disposable thermometer	4 tympanic thermometer

37°C = 98.6°F

2 Work in pairs. Practise saying these temperatures to your partner. What is normal body temperature?

1	36.6°C	3	37.4°C	5	37°C
2	35.2°C	4	38.3°C	6	37.9°C

thirty-six point six degrees

Pronunciation

3 ▶ 🔊 15 Work in pairs. Underline the stressed syllable in each word. Then listen, check your answers and repeat.

1	oral	3	electronic	5	temperature
2	tympanic	4	thermometer	6	disposable

Listening

4 ▶ 🔊 16 Listen to a nurse taking a patient's temperature and tick ✓ the words you hear.

☐ arm ☐ head ☐ mouth
☐ temperature chart ☐ thermometer ☐ tongue

5 Work in pairs. Look at the illustrations (A–E) of a nurse taking a patient's temperature and put them in the correct order (1–5).

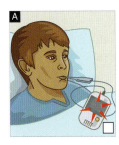
A

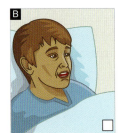
B

C

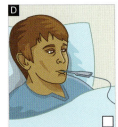
D

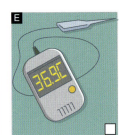
E

6 Listen again and check your answers in 5. Then complete the nurse's requests.

1 _____ you _____ your mouth for me, please?
2 _____ you just _____ this under your tongue?
3 _____ you _____ your mouth and hold for a minute?
4 _____ I just _____ out the thermometer?

Language

Making polite requests	
We use **Can/Could you** + infinitive when we ask somebody to do something for us.	**Can you** open your mouth, please? **Could you** lift up your arm for me, please?

7 Rewrite these sentences to make polite requests.

1 Put the thermometer under your tongue.
2 Hold your arm up.
3 Close your mouth.
4 Put your head to one side.
5 Take off your shirt.

Speaking **8** Work in pairs. Roleplay taking your partner's temperature.

Reading **9** Read this advice page from a health website for patients. Are the sentences *true* (T) or *false* (F)? Correct the false sentences.

Hypothermia

What is hypothermia?
Hypothermia is a very low body temperature of 35.4°C or lower. It is a serious condition that can be fatal. (Hyperthermia is a very high temperature.)

Treating hypothermia
Hypothermia is a medical emergency. Call 999 immediately. While you wait for the emergency services, you can:

• take off the patient's clothes if they are wet.
• give the patient extra clothing and/or a hat.
• cover the patient with a blanket.
• prepare a warm (not hot) drink for the patient.
• close all windows and doors.
• turn up the room temperature.
• wash the patient's hands and face in warm (not hot) water.

1 The medical term for low body temperature is *hyperthermia*. (T / F)
2 It is not necessary to call the emergency services. (T / F)
3 It is possible to die from hypothermia. (T / F)
4 A blanket will help a person with hypothermia. (T / F)
5 It is not a good idea to give the patient a very hot drink. (T / F)

Speaking **10** Work in pairs. Practise advising someone over the phone how to treat hypothermia. Use the information in 9 and the language in the Language box to make polite requests.

Can you cover the patient with a blanket, please?

The patient ward

Vocabulary **1** Work in pairs. Label this floor plan of a patient ward with the words in the box.

clean supply room   conference room   nurses' lounge   nurses' station
patient room   physicians' area   soiled utility room   visitors' toilet

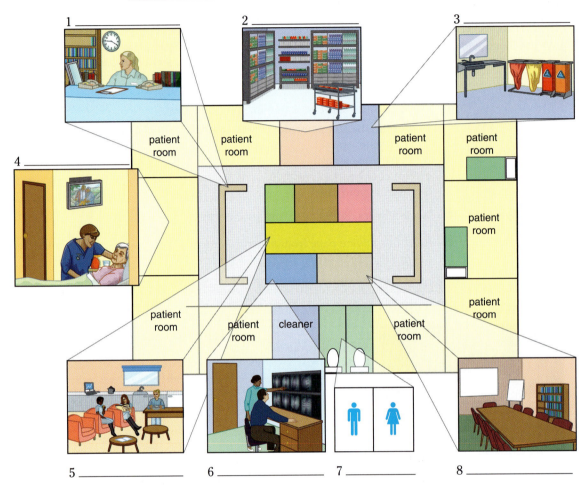

Pronunciation **2** ▶ 🔊 **17** Underline the stressed syllables in each of the sections of the patient ward in 1. Then listen, check your answers and repeat.

Language

Prepositions of place	
We use **prepositions of place** (*at*, *on*, *in*, *under*, *next to*, *near*, *down*, etc.) to say where something is.	Your father's room is **down** the hall. The nurses' station is **on** the left/right. The physicians' area is **next to** the conference room.

3 Choose the correct words in *italics*.

1 The nurses' lounge is *in* / *on* the left.
2 The clean supply room is *next* / *near* to the soiled utility room.
3 The meeting room isn't *in* / *on* this floor.
4 The conference room is *down* / *under* the hall, *at* / *on* your right.
5 Dr Evans is *in* / *on* the physicians' area.

Language

There is/There are
We use **there is/there are** to say that somebody or something exists.

Affirmative	**There's** (**is**) a thermometer in the clean supply room. (singular)
	There are two beds in the patient room. (plural)
Negative	**There isn't** (**is not**) a bandage on his leg. (singular)
	There aren't (**are not**) any clean blankets in the soiled utility room. (plural)
Question	**Is there** a toilet in the ward? (singular) Yes, **there is.**/No, **there isn't** (**is not**).
	Are there any blankets in the clean supply room? (plural) Yes, **there are.**/No, **there aren't** (**are not**).

4 Complete these sentences with the correct form of *there is* or *there are*.

1 _____ a conference room next to the physicians' area. (✓)
2 _____ two visitors' toilets down the hall. (✓)
3 _____ an X-ray machine in the physicians' area?
4 _____ a soiled utility room next to the patient room. (✗)
5 _____ two beds in Mr Rabine's room?
6 _____ any bandages in the clean supply room. (✗)

Listening **5** ▶ 🎧 18 Steve and Kelly work in different hospitals. Listen to them talking about their workplaces and tick ✓ the rooms in each workplace.

Room	Kelly's workplace	Steve's workplace
conference room		
nurses' station		
patient room		
nurses' lounge		
visitors' toilet		

6 Listen again and answer these questions.

1 What two things does Kelly like about her new job?
2 How many patient rooms are there in Steve's ward?
3 Are there any conference rooms in Kelly's ward?
4 How many nurses' stations are there in Steve's ward?
5 What can you find in the nurses' lounge in Steve's ward?

Speaking **7** Work in pairs. Ask your partner questions about a patient department he/she knows. Then swap roles and repeat the activity.

A: *Is there a conference room?*
B: *Yes, there is.*
A: *Where is it?*
B: *It's next to the physicians' area.*

Nursing duties

Speaking **1** Work in pairs. Describe what you can see in the illustrations.

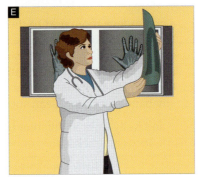

Language

Present continuous	
We use the **present continuous** to talk about things that are happening now. We use the form *am/is/are* + *-ing*.	*I'm* (*am*) *waiting* for Nurse Bower. *He's* (*is*) *helping* a patient. *We're* (*are*) *having* lunch. *The nurse is looking* for a thermometer. *What is she doing* at the moment?

2 Work in pairs. Look at the illustrations in 1. What is each person doing? Use the correct present continuous form of the verbs in the box to write a sentence for each one.

> eat   fill in   look at   look for   read   take   talk (to)

3 Complete these conversations with the correct present continuous form of the verbs in brackets.

1 A: Lisa, I need some help. (1) _____ (you / do) anything important?
   B: Yes, I'm sorry. I (2) _____ (change) Ms Bandine's IV. Is it urgent?
   A: No, I can wait five minutes.

2 A: Mr Halpert's call light is on.
   B: He (3) _____ (probably / complain) about pain again.
   A: The poor guy (4) _____ (have) trouble sleeping. I'll go and give him some pain medication.

3 A: What (5) _____ (the nursing assistants / do)?
   B: They're with Ms Davis. I think they (6) _____ (take) her temperature.

4 Work in pairs. Point to four different people in the illustrations in 1 and ask your partner what they are doing. Use the verbs in the box in 2 and *at the moment, now* and *currently*. Then swap roles and repeat the activity.

A: What is he doing?
B: He's …

Language

Present continuous for future arrangements	
We also use the **present continuous** to talk about future arrangements.	*I'm (am)* **seeing** the consultant about Mr Singh later today. *He's (is)* **consulting** the patient at 3 p.m. *We're (are)* **having** a handover meeting at 5 p.m. The consultant **is coming** to check on the patient tonight.

5 Read this email and underline the verbs in the present continuous.

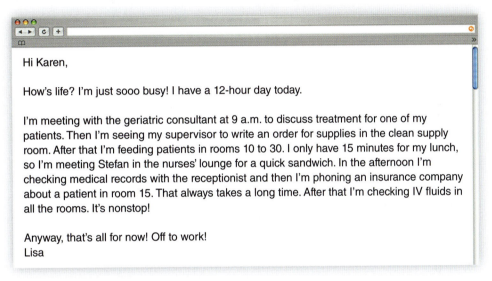

Hi Karen,

How's life? I'm just sooo busy! I have a 12-hour day today.

I'm meeting with the geriatric consultant at 9 a.m. to discuss treatment for one of my patients. Then I'm seeing my supervisor to write an order for supplies in the clean supply room. After that I'm feeding patients in rooms 10 to 30. I only have 15 minutes for my lunch, so I'm meeting Stefan in the nurses' lounge for a quick sandwich. In the afternoon I'm checking medical records with the receptionist and then I'm phoning an insurance company about a patient in room 15. That always takes a long time. After that I'm checking IV fluids in all the rooms. It's nonstop!

Anyway, that's all for now! Off to work!
Lisa

6 Are these sentences about the *present* (P) or the *future* (F)?

1 Next week I'm working the afternoon shift. (P / F)
2 Lea Thibault in room 19 is going home later today. (P / F)
3 They're currently checking temperature charts. (P / F)
4 We're meeting at the nurses' station at 5.20 for the handover. (P / F)
5 I'm looking for more bandages. Can you help me? (P / F)
6 Ken's eating his lunch in the nurses' lounge at the moment. (P / F)

Writing **7** Is Lisa's day like your day? Write an email to another nurse about what you are doing today. Use some of the verbs you underlined in 5.

Speaking **8** Work in pairs. Describe your day to your partner without looking at the email you wrote.

The qualities of a responsible nurse

Speaking **1** Work in pairs. Look at the illustration and discuss these questions.

1 What is the nurse doing?
2 What do you think the patient wants? Make a list.
3 Why is it important to always answer a call light?

Listening **2** ▶ 🔊 19 Listen to three conversations and complete these sentences with the phrases in the box.

| more pain medication   some water   to go to the toilet   to turn off the TV |

1 Mrs Azziza wants _____ .
2 Jerome wants _____ and for the nurse _____ .
3 Mr Patel needs _____ .

3 Listen again and complete the nurses' expressions.

1 _____ can I help you?
2 _____ can I do to help?
3 _____ I help you _____ anything else?
4 I'm _____ in a few _____ .

Vocabulary **4** Match 1–5 to a–e to make expressions to calm a patient.

1 ☐ Its OK, I'm   a) good hands.
2 ☐ Please try   b) care of you.
3 ☐ You're in   c) here.
4 ☐ The doctor   d) to relax.
5 ☐ We're taking   e) is coming in a few minutes.

Listening **5** ▶ 🔊 20 Listen to a nurse answering a call light. Tick ✓ the expressions in 4 that she uses.

6 Listen again and choose the correct words in *italics*.

1 Mr Friedricks can't *breathe / sleep / read*.
2 Nurse Henshaw gives him some *water / oxygen / pain medication*.
3 The nurse tries to make the patient feel *hot / tired / relaxed*.
4 The patient starts to *breathe more easily / sleep / watch TV*.

Language

Be + adjective	
We use **be** + **adjective** to describe people or things.	*The nurse **is/isn't caring**.*
Adjectives usually come after *be* or before a noun.	*Nurse Jakes **is/isn't friendly**.* *She's a **friendly nurse**.*
An adjective is the same for singular and plural nouns.	*an **attentive** nurse* ***attentive** nurses*
We can form negative adjectives with *in-*, *un-* or *im-*.	*Your nurse is **un**caring.*

7 Read these comments that patients made about their nurses. Are they *positive* (P) or *negative* (N)?

1 She never listens. I want a nurse who is attentive. (P / N)
2 The nurses in Central Hospital are always caring and patient. They take time to sit and talk to us, even when it's really busy. (P / N)
3 He's really well-informed about medicine. I think that's important – you know you're in good hands. (P / N)
4 One of the nurses is just so unfriendly. He never smiles and he's not very polite either. He often shouts at the patients. (P / N)
5 Nurse Mukherji is very flexible and she changes her routine when her patients need her. (P / N)

Vocabulary

8 Make these adjectives negative. Use *in-*, *un-* or *-im*.

1 _____ attentive
2 _____ friendly
3 _____ caring
4 _____ informed
5 _____ flexible
6 _____ polite

9 Complete this article with adjectives from 8. Use the positive or negative form. Then underline at least four more adjectives.

> ### The qualities of a responsible nurse
>
> Patients have more contact with nurses than any other member of the hospital team. To be a good nurse, you need two main qualities: you need good communication skills and you need to be well-(1) _____ about your subject. Listening is a useful communication skill and you need to be (2) _____ and really listen to your patient. They might tell you something that is important for their treatment. Responsible nurses show that they care. A(n) (3) _____ nurse means an unhappy patient. A good nurse is never (4) _____ . You may be busy but always try to smile and be (5) _____ to your patients and their visitors. A good nurse must be (6) _____ because you never know what new things you may have to do.

Speaking 10 Work in pairs. Look at the illustration. What does the patient see? Describe the two nurses to your partner. Use adjectives from 7, 8 and 9.

4

Food and measurements

- describe hospital food and beverage
- express measurements and quantitie
- help a patient order from a hospital menu
- assist a patient at mealtimes

Hospital food and beverages

Vocabulary

1 Work in pairs. Look at the illustrations of main dishes in this hospital menu and complete it with the words in the box.

> cheese omelette   grilled salmon   pizza   roast chicken
> spaghetti bolognaise   turkey sandwich   vegetable quiche

Menu
Main dishes

GH

A

B

C

D

E

F

G

2 Work in pairs. Write the words for food and beverages in the box in the correct group. Then add two items to each group.

> apple   apple juice   apple purée   banana   carrots   coffee   cola   corn
> cranberry juice   fruit salad   mashed potatoes   orange   orange juice   peas
> peppers   rice   tea   yoghurt

Side dishes	Desserts	Beverages

3 Compare your answers in 2 with another pair. Then add another two items to each group.

Language

A/An, some

We use **a/an** with singular countable nouns.	**a** carrot **an** apple
We use **a** with nouns that start with a consonant (e.g. *b, c, d, f*).	**a** potato
We use **an** with nouns that start with a vowel (*a, e, i, o, u*).	**an** orange
We use **some** with plural countable nouns, to mean 'a number of'.	**some** apples
We use **some** with uncountable nouns (nouns that exist as a mass) to mean 'a quantity of'.	**some** apple juice

Listening **4** ▶ 🎧 **21** Listen to two patients ordering food from a hospital menu and tick ✓ the food and beverage(s) they want. Then write *a, an* or *some*.

1 ☐ _____ cheese omelette   ☐ _____ mashed potatoes
   ☐ _____ coffee   ☐ _____ orange
   ☐ _____ corn   ☐ _____ peas
   ☐ _____ fruit salad   ☐ _____ piece of quiche

2 ☐ _____ apple   ☐ _____ cranberry juice
   ☐ _____ apple juice   ☐ _____ salmon
   ☐ _____ apple purée   ☐ _____ spaghetti bolognaise
   ☐ _____ banana   ☐ _____ turkey sandwich
   ☐ _____ cola   ☐ _____ yoghurt

Language

Like, would like

We use **like** to say what we always prefer.	I **like** apple juice but I **don't like** orange juice.
We use **would like** (+ *to*-infinitive) to say what we want now.	I **would** (**'d**) **like** some quiche, please. **Would you like to order** your meal now? Yes, I **would**.

5 Complete these questions and answers with the words in the box.

> do   for   like   maybe   please   to order   what   would (x3)

1 When would you like _____ your next meal? ___
2 Do you _____ roast chicken? ___
3 What would you like _____ dessert? ___
4 _____ would your visitors like to drink? ___
5 _____ they like cranberry juice? ___

a) I _____ like a banana, please.
b) They'd like coffee, _____ .
c) Yes, I think they _____ .
d) Yes, I _____ .
e) Not right now. _____ later.

6 Match questions 1–5 to answers a–e in 5.

Speaking **7** Work in pairs. Student A, you are a nurse. Help Student B choose food and beverages from 1, 2 and 4. Student B, you are a patient. Order your meal. Then swap roles and repeat the activity.

A: What would you like for your main course/dessert?   *B: I'd like …*
A: Would you like a side dish?   *B: Yes, please./No, thank you.*

Measurements and quantities

Numbers	
We say **numbers** like this:	2.45: two point four five 189: one/a hundred and eighty-nine 956: nine hundred and fifty-six 5,120: five thousand, one hundred and twenty 7,396: seven thousand, three hundred and ninety-six

Listening **1** ▶ 🔊 22 Listen and circle the numbers you hear.

1 *160 / 116*   4 *1,200 / 1,300*
2 *190 / 119*   5 *80 / 18*
3 *1,015 / 1,050*   6 *1.25 / 125*

2 Work in pairs. Write the numbers in words. Then practise saying the numbers in 1 and 2 to your partner.

1 1,200 _____   4 3,450 _____
2 2,500 _____   5 5.66 _____
3 1.76 _____   6 8.17 _____

3 ▶ 🔊 23 Listen to four conversations in which people talk about calories and write the energy values.

1 _____ calories
2 _____ calories
3 _____ calories
4 _____ calories

Vocabulary **4** Match the things nurses write (1–6) to what they say (a–f) and what each measurement measures (i–iii).

What we write	What we say	What we measure
1 ml	a) kilojoule(s)	i) weight
2 kg	b) litre(s)	ii) liquids
3 kJ	c) calories	iii) energy
4 l	d) kilogram(s)/kilo(s)	
5 g	e) gram(s)	
6 kcal	f) millilitre(s)	

5 Write sentences using the information in 4.

Nurses use millilitres to measure liquids.

Pronunciation **6** ▶ 🔊 24 Work in pairs. Underline the stressed syllable in each word. Then listen, check your answers and repeat.

1 kilo   4 kilojoule
2 calorie   5 kilogram
3 litre   6 millilitre

Language

Metric conversions	
1 fl oz (fluid ounce) = 29.574 ml	1 oz (ounce) = 28.35 g
35.195 fl oz = 1 litre (1,000 ml)	1 lb (pound) = 0.4536 kg

7 Listen to track 23 again and choose the correct words in *italics*.

1 How *much / many* glasses of orange juice can I order?
2 How *much / many* apple purée do you want?
3 How *much / many* milk can I have, Nurse Webster?
4 Can you tell me how *much / many* calories Mrs Kelly is allowed?

Language

How much/How many, much/many	
We use **how much** and **much** to talk about quantities we can't count.	**How much** milk can I have? He doesn't have **much** time.
We use **how many** and **many** to talk about quantities we can count.	**How many** apples can you eat? There aren't **many** oranges left.

8 A student nurse (SN) is asking a nurse (N) about the clear liquid diet. Complete their conversation with *much* and *many*.

SN: I don't know (1) _____ about the clear liquid diet. Can you explain it to me?

N: Yeah, of course. It's a diet of clear liquids. Patients can digest these easily, so we give it to them after an operation, for example.

SN: I see. For how (2) _____ days?

N: Not more than three days, and then we put them on a full liquid diet. For the clear liquid diet, patients can drink (3) _____ different kinds of liquid.

SN: So how (4) _____ do patients drink in one day on this diet?

N: For some patients, not more than 600 ml. We encourage others to drink as much as possible.

SN: How (5) _____ calories in total?

N: Well, it depends. But remember: water, black coffee and tea have zero calories but there are 255 calories in a glass of cranberry juice.

9 Work in pairs. Practise the conversation in 8.

Speaking **10** Work in pairs. Put a cross ✗ for the items that are not part of the clear liquid diet.

Patient name:	*Ivy Manning*		
	Amount (ml)		**Amount (ml)**
☐ Black coffee	*0 (2 cups)*	☐ Popsicles (ice)	*100 (2)*
☐ Bouillon	*150 (1 bowl)*	☐ Tea with lemon	*0 (2 ½ cups)*
☐ Cranberry juice	*240 (1 glass)*	☐ Tea with milk	*360 (3 cups)*
☐ Ice cream	*150 (1 bowl)*	☐ Tomato soup	*150 (1 bowl)*
☐ Milk	*360 (1 ½ glasses)*	☐ Vegetable soup	*150 (1 bowl)*
☐ Orange juice	*360 (1 ½ glasses)*	**Total:** _____ ml	

11 Work in pairs. Student A, you are a nurse. Choose five items from 10. Then ask Student B, a nutritionist, what the patient, Ivy Manning, usually eats/drinks. Student B, answer Student A's questions.

A: How much ... does Mrs Manning usually drink?
B: She usually drinks ... ml of ... .

12 Work in the same pairs. Four days later Ivy Manning begins a full liquid diet. Student B, now you are the nurse. Choose five items from 10. Then ask Student A, the nutritionist, what the patient can eat. Student A, answer Student B's questions.

Helping a patient order from a hospital menu

Speaking **1** Work in small groups. Discuss these questions. Then present your ideas to the class.

    1 Which foods are usually given to hospital patients in your country or place of work?

    2 How much choice do patients have in your country or place of work?

Vocabulary **2** Look at these photos and complete the sentences with the verbs in the box.

| breathe   chew   drink   swallow |

1 People need air to _____ .
2 _____ your food well before you _____ it.
3 You must _____ lots of liquids when it's hot.

Reading **3** Work in pairs. Look at this hospital menu and decide what you would like to order. Then tell your partner.

Menu *Tuesday 19th October*

To order your meal, choose one item from each section.

Starters
- Chicken soup (D) ____
- Orange juice (D/V) ____

Main courses
- Grilled chicken and vegetables (D) ____
- Beef salad (D) ____
- Cheese omelette (V) ____
- Mediterranean vegetable lasagne (D/V) ____
- Tomato & mozzarella salad (V) ____

Side dishes
- Mashed potatoes (V) ____
- Rice (D/V) ____
- Bread roll & butter/sunflower spread (D/V) ____

Desserts
- Fresh fruit salad (D/V) ____
- Ice cream (D/V) ____
- Cherry tart (V) ____
- Yoghurt and honey (D) ____

Codes: V = vegetarian; D = diabetic; S = soft

Listening **4** ▶ 🎧 25 Cherif and Lydia are ordering their dinner. Listen and write *C* (Cherif) or *L* (Lydia) next to the food they order from the menu in 3.

5 Work in pairs. Listen again and correct these sentences. Then compare your answers with your partner.

Cherif has problems breathing.
Cherif has problems swallowing.

    1 The lasagne is made of beef, tomatoes and pasta with a cheese sauce.
    2 Cherif would like cherry tart for dessert.
    3 Lydia doesn't like vegetables.
    4 She orders a cheese omelette and a bread roll with butter for the main course.
    5 She would like yoghurt for dessert and a glass of orange juice for the starter.

6 Put the words in 1–4 in the correct order to make the patients' questions.

1 I have problems swallowing. / you / do / what / suggest / ?
2 vegetable lasagne / made / what's / the / of / ?
3 have / can / today / I'm / what / I / so / a vegetarian, / ?
4 I / the cherry tart / am / to eat / allowed / ?

7 Complete the nurse's answers to the questions in 6.

1 _____ a cheese omelette?
2 _____ tomatoes and peppers with pasta and a cheese sauce.
3 _____ some lasagne or the tomato and mozzarella salad?
4 _____ you're on a restricted diet for the next few days, Lydia.

8 Look at the audio script for track 25 on page 75 and check your answers in 6 and 7.

Speaking

9 Work in small groups. Look at the menu in 3 and add the code *S* (soft diet) to the correct foods. Compare your ideas with the rest of the class.

10 Lara is ordering her lunch from the menu in 3. Complete her conversation with the nurse.

A soft diet consists of food that is easy to swallow.

Diabetes (adjective: *diabetic*) is a disease where there is too much sugar in the blood.

Lara – diabetic diet

Jaroslav – vegetarian diet

Wesley – soft diet

Nurse: (1) _____ order for your lunch today, Lara?
Lara: I'm diabetic, so what do you suggest?
Nurse: (2) _____ the chicken and vegetables?
Lara: Maybe. What's in it?
Nurse: (3) _____ grilled chicken served with broccoli and green peppers.
Lara: That sounds nice. OK, I'll have that.
Nurse: (4) _____ a side dish?
Lara: What can I have?
Nurse: (5) _____ some rice?
Lara: OK. Am I allowed to have a dessert?
Nurse: Yes, of course. (6) _____ fresh fruit salad, ice cream or yoghurt and honey?
Lara: I'd like some ice cream, please. Thanks.
Nurse: Great. I'll hand in your menu card for you.

11 Work in pairs. Practise the conversation in 10. Then swap roles and repeat the activity.

12 1 Work in pairs. Student A, you are a nurse. Take Jaroslav's order from the menu in 3. Student B, you are Jaroslav. Order lunch from the menu in 3.

2 Swap roles. Student B, now you are the nurse. Take Wesley's order. Student A, you are Wesley. Order lunch from the menu in 3.

Assisting the patient at mealtimes

Vocabulary   **1**   Match the words in the box to these definitions.

> non-slip mat   non-slip plate   plastic apron   straw   two-handled cup

1   Nurses can use it to cover their clothes. _____
2   Patients put it into a cup or glass and use it for drinking. _____
3   It doesn't move, so it is easier for patients to eat from it. _____
4   We use it to stop plates moving on the tray table. _____
5   Patients can hold it with both hands and drink from it. _____

Reading   **2**   Look at the title of this text. How would you help a patient to eat?

Assisting a patient at mealtimes

It is important to give patients help (if necessary) and encouragement at mealtimes as good **nutrition** helps patients **recover** more quickly.

A _____

A patient is more likely to want to eat if he or she is clean, comfortable and relaxed. Help patients to:

- go to the toilet, wash their hands and brush their teeth.
- sit **upright** in bed or a chair.

You should also:

- put the **tray table** at the right height for the patient.
- cut up food into small pieces.
- give non-slip mats and two-handled cups, etc. (if necessary).

B _____

- Sit in front of the patient and **make eye contact**.
- Give small portions and stop for a minute after each **mouthful**.
- Give a drink after each mouthful (if necessary).

C _____

It is important that patients try and eat something – even if it's just a little. You could:

- smile and be friendly.
- say **positive** things about the food.

3   Read the text in 2 and choose the correct subheading for each section (A–C) from the box.

> Encouraging the patient   Helping the patient to eat   Preparing the patient to eat

4   Match the words in **bold** in the text in 2 to these definitions.

1   good _____
2   get better after an illness or accident _____
3   a type of table that people use so that they can eat in bed _____
4   an amount of food or drink that you put into your mouth at one time _____
5   food and drink for good health and growth _____
6   look directly at someone at the same time as they are looking at you _____
7   sitting straight up _____
8   helping someone to do something _____

Listening **5** Look at the photo. What is the nurse doing?

6 ▶ 🔊 26 Nurse Paula Minelli is helping Mrs Taylor. Listen and complete these expressions.
1 Would you like _____ with your meal today?
2 Would you like _____ for your orange juice?
3 You're _____ well.
4 How about _____ orange juice?
5 That's _____ .
6 Just _____ potato?

7 Work in pairs. Listen again and answer these questions.
1 Why does Mrs Taylor want the nurse to help her?
2 What is Mrs Taylor eating?
3 Why doesn't Mrs Taylor want to eat?
4 How does the nurse encourage Mrs Taylor to eat?

8 Look at the audio script for track 26 on pages 75–76 and find an example of something positive the nurse says about the food.

Language **9** Are these expressions used to *encourage* (E) a patient or *praise* (P) him/her?
1 Could you just try a little ...? (E / P)
2 Well done. (E / P)
3 That's good. (E / P)
4 Can you just try a little more ...? (E / P)

10 Which expressions in 6 are used to encourage patients? Which are used to praise patients?

11 Look at the audio script for track 26 on pages 75–76 again and underline all the expressions of praise and encouragement the nurse uses.

Speaking **12** Work in small groups. Read this case study. What could a nurse do to help the patient at mealtimes?

> **Case study**
> Anja Radejevic, 46, is visually impaired. She is on a soft diet after a hip replacement operation. She doesn't like fruit or cheese.

13 Put the words in the correct order to make a useful expression to help the patient find food on the plate.

at twelve o'clock / the potatoes / are / at six o'clock / and the beans / are

14 Work in pairs. Student A, you are Anja. Choose items from the hospital menu on page 32. Student B, you are a nurse. Assist Anja with her meal. Use expressions from 6 and 9 and remember to encourage and praise the patient. Then swap roles and repeat the activity.

The body and movement

- **the body: limbs and joints**
- **the body: torso and head**
- **set goals and give encouragement**
- **document Range of Motion (ROM) exercises**

The body: limbs and joints

Vocabulary

1 Label the parts of the body in this illustration with the words in the box.

> arm   finger   foot   hand   heel   leg   thumb   toe

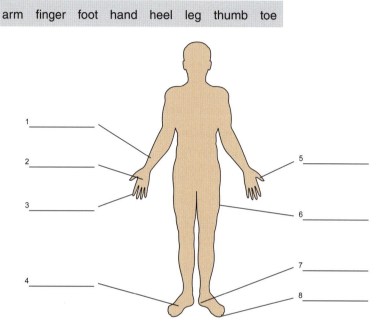

1 _____
2 _____
3 _____
4 _____
5 _____
6 _____
7 _____
8 _____

2 Circle the joints in the illustration in 1. Then label them with the words in the box.

> ankle   elbow   hip   knee   shoulder   wrist

Listening

3 ▶ 🔘 27   Listen to a conversation between a nurse and a patient and tick ✓ the parts of the body you hear.

☐ arm   ☐ foot   ☐ leg
☐ knee   ☐ hand   ☐ thumb
☐ finger   ☐ heel   ☐ toe

4 Listen again. Which body parts does the nurse tell the patient to:
1 push?   3 lift?
2 rotate?   4 bend?

Language

Imperative	
We use **the imperative** (infinitive without *to*) to tell somebody to do something or give them instructions.	**Lift** *your leg.* **Push** *the chair.* **Bend** *your arm.* **Rotate** *your hand.*

Speaking **5** Work in pairs. Practise giving a patient simple instructions. Use the verbs in the Language box and the words in 1 and 2. Your partner should follow the instructions. Then swap roles and repeat the activity.

Lift your hand.
Bend your arm.

Reading **6** Read this brochure and write the correct exercise in each space (1–5).

Exercises for recovery

Regular exercises are important to help you after surgery. Your orthopaedic surgeon and physical therapist may recommend that you exercise 20 to 30 minutes, two or three times a day.

standing knee bends

(1) _____
In bed, slowly push your foot up and down. Repeat several times a day. You can do this exercise immediately after surgery.

ankle rotations

(2) _____
Keep your heel on the bed and bend your knee. Then straighten your leg again. Repeat ten times, three or four times a day.

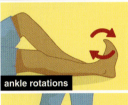

leg lifts

(3) _____
Move your ankle in a circular motion. Repeat five times in each direction, three or four times a day.

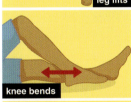

knee bends

(4) _____
Move your leg out to the side as far as you can and then back. Repeat ten times, three or four times a day.

ankle pumps

(5) _____
Stand up and lift your knee, but not too high. Hold for two or three seconds. Repeat ten times, three or four times a day.

7 Read the brochure in 6 again and answer these questions.

1 Which exercise can patients do immediately after an operation?
2 How long is each exercise session?
3 Find the names of two medical professionals and underline the stressed syllables.

Speaking **8** Work in pairs. Student A, give Student B instructions for exercises for his/her arm, foot, leg and hand. Student B, follow Student A's instructions. Then swap roles. Student B, give Student A instructions for exercises for their ankle, hip, knee, shoulder and wrist. Student A, follow Student B's instructions. Use the verbs in the brochure in 6 and in the Language box on page 36 to help you.

The body: torso and head

Vocabulary **1** Label the parts of the body in illustrations A and B with the words in the box.

| back | buttocks | chest | face | head | hip | neck | shoulder | stomach | waist |

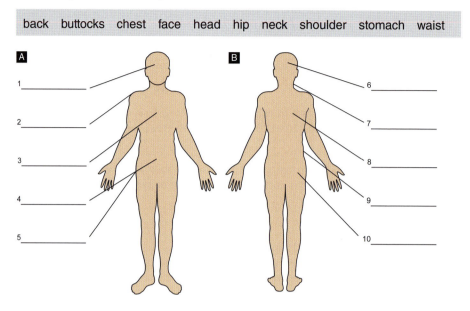

A

1 _____

2 _____

3 _____

4 _____

5 _____

B

6 _____

7 _____

8 _____

9 _____

10 _____

Language

Prepositions of place and movement	
We use **prepositions of place** to say where something is.	The chair is **in front of** you.
We use **prepositions of movement** to say in which direction something is moving.	Lift **up** your arm above your head. Push **down** with your hand. Move your leg **to** the side/**to** the left/**to** the right.

2 Complete this conversation between Nurse Naughton (N) and Ms Duggan (D), a patient, with *up*, *down*, *above* and *in front of*.

N: Morning, Ms Duggan. Are you ready for your exercise session today?

D: I'm a little tired this morning but I'll try.

N: Good to hear that. We're going to try some new exercises today to help you walk.

D: OK. The old exercises were a little too easy.

N: Well, that's good news. Now, first, I'll put the chair (1) _____ you. Hold it. Good. Now lift (2) _____ your right knee – not too high. Yes, just there. Don't lift it (3) _____ your waist.

D: Can I put it (4) _____? It hurts.

N: Yes, that's OK. Put your leg (5) _____ . That's good. Now repeat that five times. Let's count together. One, two, three; that's very good. Well done! How do you feel?

D: Not so bad. It's tough at first, especially the left leg, but I can feel I'm getting stronger.

Reading **3** Read the conversation in 2 again and answer these questions.

1 How does Ms Duggan feel this morning?

2 What does she think about the old exercises?

3 Does she start with the left or right leg?

4 What does she think of the new exercises?

Speaking   **4**   Work in pairs. Student A, look at the information on this page. Student B, look at the information on page 70. Follow the instructions.

Student A

Call Student B and ask questions to complete the Range of Motion (ROM) exercise record for a patient, Mr Ahmad.

Movement	Repetitions	Comments	Nurse initials

Which ROM exercises does Mr Ahmad need to do?
How many repetitions?
Are there any comments?

Vocabulary   **5**   Match the verbs (1–5) to their opposites (a–e).

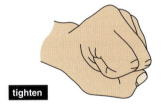
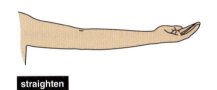
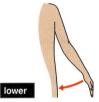

1   tighten   a)   stand up
2   bend   b)   lower
3   push   c)   straighten
4   sit down   d)   pull
5   lift   e)   relax

Language

When + clause + it helps

We use **when + clause + it helps** to explain the benefits of exercise to a patient.	**When you bend your fingers**, **it helps** the muscles in your wrist. **When I hold your head**, **it helps** your neck. **When you touch your toes**, **it helps** the muscles in your back. **When you do your exercises**, **it helps** you recover from surgery.

6   Use these prompts to write sentences about the benefits of exercise. Use *when* + clause + *it helps*.

lift / your chest – your back
When you lift your chest, it helps your back.

1   rotate / your shoulder – the muscles in your neck
2   bend / your waist – your hips
3   do / your exercises – you / recover from surgery faster
4   hold / a chair in front of you – you / balance

Speaking   **7**   Work in pairs. Student A, help Student B to do exercises for the waist, neck, shoulders and head. Use the verbs in 5 and *when* + clause + *it helps*. Student B, follow Student A's instructions. Then swap roles. Student B, help Student A to do exercises for the hips, chest and back. Student A, follow Student B's instructions.

Setting goals and giving encouragement

Speaking **1** What are the patients in illustrations A–C thinking? Match sentences 1–3 to patients A–C.

1 I just want to be able to eat my breakfast.
2 I want to climb the stairs alone.
3 I want to put my clothes on by myself.

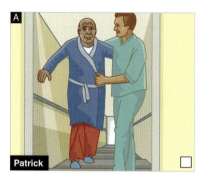

A Patrick ☐

B Hugo ☐

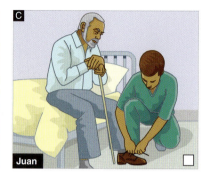

C Juan ☐

2 Work in pairs. Think of one or more ROM exercise(s) for each patient in 1.

Patrick wants to ..., so he needs to exercise his ...

Listening **3** 🔊 **28** Put the words in 1–6 in the correct order to make sentences and questions. Then listen to the three patients in 1 and check your answers.

1 what's / goal / long-term / your / ?
2 you / want / today / to do / what / do / ?
3 you / what / do / can / ?
4 three sets of ten / for today / on each arm / our goal is
5 that / can / you / do / ?
6 this exercise / three times / do / a day / can you / ?

Pronunciation **4** 🔊 **29** Listen and underline the stressed word in each question. Then listen again and repeat.

In English we often stress the words in a sentence that we think are important.

1 What do you want to do today?
2 Can you do this exercise three times a day?
3 What can you do?
4 Can you do that?

5 Work in pairs. Look at the audio script for track 28 on page 76 and practise the conversations. Remember to stress the underlined words.

Language

Comparative adjectives	
One-syllable adjectives: add *-er/-r*.	*high – high**er***
Adjectives ending in *-y*: change *-y* to *-i* and add *-er*.	*easy – easi**er***
Adjectives of two or more syllables: add *more*.	*difficult – **more** difficult*
Good/well and *bad* are irregular.	*good/well – **better*** *bad – **worse***
We use **comparative adjectives** to compare two people or things. We often use **than** after the comparative adjective.	*Exercises become **easier** when you do them regularly.* *This exercise is **better than** that one.*

well = healthy

6 Complete these sentences with the comparative form of the adjectives in brackets.

1 Do the muscles in your arm feel _____ (strong) after the exercise sessions?
2 Thanks, I feel much _____ (good) today.
3 Excellent, Mr Elliot! That's _____ (high) than yesterday.
4 Can we stop, please? The pain is getting _____ (bad).
5 I find the ROM exercises _____ (easy) now than three weeks ago.
6 It's _____ (difficult) to lift my left leg than my right leg. There's still a lot of pain.
7 I see you're _____ (well) today; that's great.
8 I think Tilly's movements are _____ (slow) this afternoon after the medication.

Writing **7** Complete this 'pain diary' of one of the patients in 1 with the comparative form of the adjectives in the box.

> bad   difficult   easy (x2)   good   strong

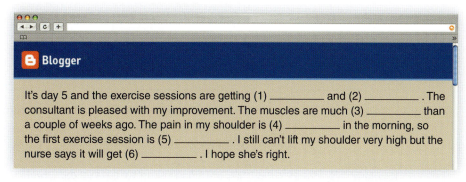

It's day 5 and the exercise sessions are getting (1) _____ and (2) _____ . The consultant is pleased with my improvement. The muscles are much (3) _____ than a couple of weeks ago. The pain in my shoulder is (4) _____ in the morning, so the first exercise session is (5) _____ . I still can't lift my shoulder very high but the nurse says it will get (6) _____ . I hope she's right.

8 Who writes this blog, Patrick, Juan or Hugo?

Listening **9** ▶ 🔊 30 Listen to a nurse working with Thelma, a patient, on her recovery exercises. Are these sentences *true* (T) or *false* (F)? Correct the false sentences.

1 Thelma's goal is four sets of five on each leg. (T / F)
2 It is more difficult to move the left leg. (T / F)
3 The nurse asks Thelma to do leg lifts. (T / F)
4 Thelma repeats the exercise three times on the left leg. (T / F)
5 Thelma says she's in a lot of pain. (T / F)

10 Listen again and complete the nurse's expressions of encouragement.

1 That's _____ .
2 You're doing _____ .
3 That's _____ .
4 _____ better, well done!

11 Look at the audio script for track 30 on page 76 and check your answers in 9 and 10.

Speaking **12** Work in pairs. Look at the audio script for track 30 on page 76 and practise the conversation. Then swap roles and repeat the activity.

13 Practise your conversations from 7 on page 39. Follow these steps.

1 Explain the benefits of the exercise.
2 Set the goals.
3 Encourage the patient.

Documenting ROM exercises

Vocabulary **1** Work in small groups. Look at illustrations A–F and brainstorm words that a nurse would use to ask a patient to make the movements.

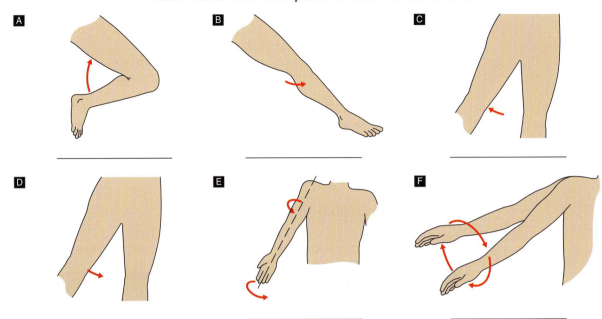

2 Work in pairs. Label illustrations A–F in 1 with the medical terms in the box.

abduction   adduction   circumduction   extension   flexion   rotation

Reading **3** Read Nurse Carter's assessment of Joe Felicie, who is in traction after a road accident. Match the words in **bold** to definitions 1–8.

> **GCH** General Central Hospital
>
> **ROM Assessment: Joe Felicie, 28 yrs**
> - pt conscious but tired, with nausea (pain medication); left shoulder: bruising and swelling
> - ROM **limited to** 100° with great **discomfort**
> - left leg **immobilised**; other joints fully **mobile**
> - health status **prior to** accident excellent; pt **unwilling** to perform ROM
>
> **Planning ROM exercises**
> - Stage 1: begin with **passive ROM** two times a day (9.00, 17.00) for first two days.
> - Stage 2: teach pt to perform **active ROM** three times a day (9.00, 12.00, 17.00).

1 before _____
2 not wanting to do something and refusing to do it _____
3 prevented from moving _____
4 exercises the patient can do by himself/herself _____
5 able to move normally _____
6 a feeling of pain or of being physically uncomfortable _____
7 prevented from increasing beyond a particular point _____
8 exercises a nurse does for the patient _____

4 Nurses often use an abbreviation for the word *patient*. What is it? Check your answer in the assessment in 3.

Vocabulary **5** Nurse Carter is explaining Joe's case to a colleague. Complete his explanation with the words in the box.

> before doesn't want left medication nauseous
> normally only pain swollen

'Joe is conscious but very tired. He also feels (1) _____ because of the (2) _____ . His (3) _____ shoulder is bruised and (4) _____ . He can (5) _____ move his shoulder to a 100° angle and he's in a lot of (6) _____ . However, he is able to move all his other joints (7) _____ . (8) _____ the accident Joe was in excellent health. He's very tired today and (9) _____ to do ROM exercises at the moment.'

Listening **6** ▶ 🔊 31 Listen and tick ✓ the ROM exercises Joe can do.

Flow sheet – range of motion exercises **GCH** *General Central Hospital*
Patient: *Joe Felicie*   **Room N°:** *214*   **Date:** *04.03.2012*

Movement	Time	Comments
	09.00	
R shoulder flexion		WNL
R shoulder rotation		WNL
R hip abduction		(1) WNL with *some / no* pain
R hip extension		(2) WNL with *some / no* pain
L shoulder flexion		(3) limited to *100° / 120°*
L shoulder extension		(4) *able / not able to do*

Nurse's initials: *RPC*

WNL = within normal limits

7 Listen again and circle the correct words in *italics* in 6 (1–4).

Speaking **8** Student A, look at the information on this page. Student B, look at the information on page 70. Follow the instructions.

Student A
Read Joe's flow sheet for 7th March and explain to Student B which exercises the patient can and can't do. Then swap roles and listen to Student B.

Flow sheet – Range of motion exercises **GCH** *General Central Hospital*
Patient: *Joe Felicie*   **Room N°:** *214*   **Date:** 07.03.2012

Movement	Time		Comments
	12.00	17.00	
R shoulder flexion	✓		WNL
R shoulder rotation	✓		WNL
R hip abduction	✓		WNL with a little pain
R hip extension	✓		WNL
L shoulder flexion	✓		WNL with some pain
L shoulder extension			limited to 90°
L hip abduction			limited to 50°
L hip extension			not able to do
L knee extension			not able to do

Nurse's initials:

Joe can bend his right shoulder normally. He can …

6 Medication

- understand medication routes and for[m]
- prepare dosages
- explain the side effects of medicatio[n]
- assist patients with medication
- communicate with relatives by phon[e]

Medication routes and forms

Speaking **1** Look at these notes and match the 'five rights' (1–5) to illustrations A–E.

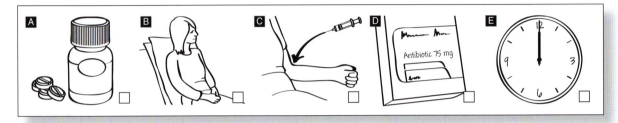

1 right patient   3 right medication   5 right route
2 right time   4 right dose

2 Work in small groups. Answer these questions.

1 Why is it important to remember the 'five rights' of medication?
2 Look at illustration C in 1. What other routes do you know? Make a list.
   muscle

Vocabulary **3** Match words 1–10 to illustrations A–J.

1 capsules   6 ointment
2 drops   7 spray
3 inhaler   8 suppository
4 injection   9 syrup
5 IV drip   10 tablets

Bains
Paracetamol
500 mg

for the relief of headache,
migraine, neuralgia, toothache,
sore throat, period pain,
rheumatic aches and pains, fever
and the symptoms of colds and flu

16 capsules

EasyEye

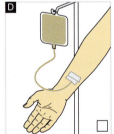

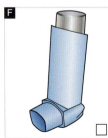
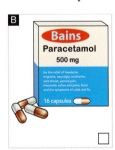

Bootle's

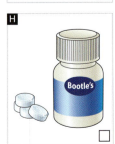

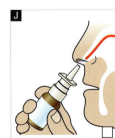

IV = intravenous
tablet = pill

4 Work in pairs. Match the forms of medication in 3 to these routes. You can use some words more than once.

1 (into the) ear _____
2 (into the) eye _____
3 (by) mouth _____
4 (into the) muscle _____
5 (into the) nose _____

6 (into the) rectum _____
7 (on the) skin _____
8 (under the) skin _____
9 (under the) tongue _____
10 (into a) vein _____

Listening **5** ▶ 🎧 32 Listen to four nurses talking about medication and tick ✓ the medical problem for each patient.

Katy Cheung

Ted Mathews

Suzanna Fox

Ali Haddad

1 Katy: ☐ heart problems ☐ ear infection ☐ nausea ☐ skin rash
2 Ted: ☐ heart problems ☐ ear infection ☐ nausea ☐ skin rash
3 Mrs Fox: ☐ heart problems ☐ ear infection ☐ nausea ☐ skin rash
4 Ali: ☐ heart problems ☐ ear infection ☐ nausea ☐ skin rash

6 Listen again and complete this table.

	Medication form	Route
Katy		
Ted		
Mrs Fox		
Ali		

7 Work in pairs. Listen again. Are these sentences *true* (T) or *false* (F)? Correct the false sentences.

1 Katy feels cold. (T / F)
2 The nurse is going to administer Ted's medication. (T / F)
3 Mrs Fox is confused about her medication. (T / F)
4 Student nurses can administer medication. (T / F)

8 Complete these explanations from the conversations in track 32 with the words in the box. Then listen again and check your answers.

a lot better   go to bed   lunchtime   right   three   two   water   25 mg   22.00

1 Please take _____ tablets now. You can swallow them with _____ .
2 That's _____ drops into his _____ ear now, Mrs Mathews, and then again just before he goes to bed.
3 You take _____ now with a glass of water. The second one at _____ , then again at around 7 p.m. And the last one when you _____ .
4 His next injection will be in the evening, at _____ .
5 His skin rash is _____ , isn't it?

Speaking **9** Work in pairs. Look at the audio script for track 32 on pages 76–77 and practise the conversations.

Dosages and frequency

Vocabulary **1** What do the symbols in the box mean? Match them to terms 1–5.

$$+ \quad \div \quad = \quad \times \quad -$$

1 minus/subtracted from ___   4 equals/is ___
2 plus/added to ___   5 divide(d) by ___
3 multiplied by/times ___

Listening **2** 🔊 **33** Work in pairs. Listen to three conversations and complete these calculations. Then practise saying them to your partner.

1 60 mg ___ 20 mg ___ 3 tablets
2 250 ml ___ 2 hours ___ 125 ml per hour
3 28 kg ___ 1.5 mg = ___ mg

Vocabulary **3** Write these calucations in words. Then practise saying them aloud.

1 100 mg + 150 mg = 250 mg _____
2 80 ml – 45 ml = 35 ml _____
3 60 mg ÷ 5 mg = 12 mg _____
4 3 × 5 ml = 15 ml _____

Language

Expressions of frequency
We can talk about frequency like this:

Take these tablets **once a day** at 8.00.
I take my iron tablets **twice a day** at 8.00 and 22.00.
He uses a suppository **every second day**/**every other day**, on Monday, Wednesday and Friday.
The nurse administers medication **three times a day**, at 8.00, 13.00 and 19.00.
We give him a morphine injection **every four hours**, at 8.00, 12.00, 16.00, 20.00, etc.

---

4 Match expressions 1–5 to patients a–e.

1 three times a day ___
2 twice a day ___
3 once a day ___
4 every four hours ___
5 every second day ___

a) Ms Ford	08.00 ✓	12.00 ✓	16.00 ✓	20.00 ✓	00.00 ✓
b) Ms Sandhu	08.00 ✓	13.00 ✓	22.00 ✓		
c) Ms O'Riley	08.00 ✓	12.00	16.00	20.00	22.00 ✓
d) Ms Meleki	08.00	13.00 ✓	16.00	20.00	22.00
e) Ms Andrews	Mon ✓	Tues	Wed ✓	Thurs	Fri ✓

Reading **5** Read the wiki entry on page 47 and answer these questions.

1 What was the language of medicine in Europe in ancient times?
2 When do medical professionals use Latin today?
3 Why did the Australian Commission on Safety and Quality in Healthcare produce a new list of medical abbreviations?

Wiki-nurse Australia

Medical terms and abbreviations for prescriptions

After the fall of the Roman Empire in the fifth century AD Latin continued to be the language of communication in Western Europe, and also of medicine. Today the language of medicine is English but medical professionals still use Latin abbreviations, especially to write prescriptions. For example, *po* means 'by mouth', *pc* means 'before meals', *ac* means 'after meals' and *hs* means 'at bedtime'. However, unless you have studied medicine, these abbreviations are not easy to understand. It is also difficult to read abbreviations when they are handwritten, and people often make mistakes. All this can cause serious patient safety issues.

In 2008 the Australian Commission on Safety and Quality in Healthcare compiled a list of terms and abbreviations that were clearer and easier to read. Here are some of the abbreviations that regularly cause problems:

Abbreviation	Meaning	Mistaken for ...	Use ...
BID or *bid*	twice a day	tid (three times a day)	bd
QD or *qd*	every day	qid (four times a day)	daily
QOD or *qod*	every other day	qd (every day) or qid	every second day
6/24	every six hours	six times a day	6 hrly
TID or *tid*	three times a day	bd	tds

Vocabulary

6 Work in pairs. Match the terms and abbreviations (1–4) to the expressions of frequency (a–d).

1 4 hrly
2 bd
3 daily
4 tds

a) once a day/every day
b) every four hours
c) twice a day
d) three times a day

Writing

7 Look at prescriptions 1–3 and find abbreviations or symbols that match these meanings.

1 after meals _____
2 at bedtime _____
3 before meals _____
4 capsules _____

5 milligrams _____
6 number _____
7 tablets _____
8 twice a day _____

1

General Central Hospital

Pt: Sally Taylor
Zocor 10 mg
one po daily hs
Dispense #90

2

General Central Hospital

Pt: Edna Cuthbert
Diovan 40 mg (tabs)
one po daily (pc/ac)
Dispense #90

3

General Central Hospital

Pt: Masoud Khan
Fluvastatin 20 mg (caps)
1 bd x 7 days
Dispense #14

8 Read the prescriptions in 7 and write them out in words.

1 You need to give Sally Taylor *ten milligrams of Zocor once a day by mouth, at bedtime* for *90 days*.
2 Diovan is for your blood pressure, Edna. _____ for _____ .
3 For your cholesterol, your doctor has prescribed Fluvastatin, Mr Khan. You need to take _____ .

Side effects; assisting patients with medication

Speaking **1** Work in pairs. Discuss these questions. Then compare your ideas with the rest of the class.

1 What are side effects of medication?
2 Make a list of five common side effects.

Listening **2** ▶ 🔊 **34** Listen to Les, a nursing lecturer, talking about side effects to a group of student nurses and tick ✓ the side effects he mentions.

☐ dizziness ☐ skin rash ☐ tremors
☐ diarrhoea ☐ stomachache ☐ constipation
☐ headaches ☐ swelling ☐ drowsiness
☐ nausea ☐ vomiting ☐ loss of appetite

3 Put the words in 1–5 in the correct order to make sentences. Then listen again and check your answers.

1 some patients / suffer / as you know, / side effects / and others don't
2 might feel nauseous / may suffer dizziness / some people / and others
3 even headaches / to have diarrhoea, / it's also possible / vomiting,
4 may cause swelling at the injection site / for some patients / injecting drugs intravenously
5 Valium / drowsiness / patients who take / may experience

Language

May, might

We use **may/might** + infinitive to talk about actions or events that are possible now or in the future.	You **may feel** some nausea. (It is possible but not 100 percent sure.) He **might suffer** some swelling from the injection. It **may take** several months to heal up completely. We **might carry out** more tests after we take off the bandages.

---

4 Use these prompts to write sentences with *may* or *might*. Put the verbs in brackets in the correct place.

1 you / a little dizzy after you take your medication (feel)
2 some patients / abdominal pains or sweating (experience)
3 your husband / some side effects but most patients don't (suffer)
4 you / some side effects to this drug (get)
5 we'll monitor him as we / to reduce his dosage (need)
6 it / a few weeks for the wound to heal completely (take)

Vocabulary **5** Look at the audio script for track 34 on page 77. Find words for side effects that match these definitions. Underline the words as you read.

1	**2**	**3**	**4**	**5**
_____:	_____:	_____:	_____:	_____:
an illness where the patient frequently passes solid waste, often in a liquid form	a condition where the patient cannot pass solid waste from the body	when the patient feels sleepy	no longer having a desire for food	shaking movements in your body that you cannot control

Speaking **6** Sometimes patients forget to take their medication. Work in pairs. What techniques can they use to help them to remember? Discuss.

take the medication at the same time of day

Reading **7** Read this patient brochure and answer the questions.

Tips for managing your medication

1 Ask questions about your medicines. Your doctor, pharmacist and nurse can help you learn about your medications and why they are important.

2 Check labels. Be sure you are taking the correct medication and have the correct dosage.

3 Avoid mistakes – don't take medication in the dark!

4 Tell your doctor if you take over-the-counter remedies such as vitamin tablets, herbal medicines and aspirin. These sometimes react with other medications.

5 Report any new side effects. You may need to take a different dosage or your doctor may decide to try a different medication.

6 Always carry a list of your medications. This is helpful to a health team in an emergency.

1 Why is it important to read the label of a medication?
2 Why is it important not to take medication in the dark?
3 Give two examples of over-the-counter medication.
4 Why is it important to tell the doctor about new side effects?
5 Why is it a good idea to carry a list of medications?

Listening **8** ▶ 🌐 35 Listen to a conversation between a nurse and Doris, a patient, and complete 1–6 in Doris' medication record. Then compare your answers with a partner.

Personal medication record			Patient: *Doris MacDonald*		GCH
					General Central Hospital
Medication	**Reason for use**	**Form**	**Route**	**How much & when?**	**Side effects**
(1) _____	*glaucoma*	_____	*right + left eye*	_____ _____	*headaches, itchy, red eyes – temporary*
insulin	(2) _____	*injection*	_____	*six units, every six hours*	_____ _____
(3) _____	(4) _____	_____	*mouth*	_____ _____	*diarrhoea*
Tamiflu	(5) _____	_____	*mouth*	_____ _____	*nausea, vomiting (take with food)*
(6) _____	*general health*	*tablets*	_____	*1 mg a day*	_____ _____

Speaking **9** Student A, look at Doris' medication record in 8. Student B, look at the information on page 71. Ask each other questions to complete the medication record.

Why is Doris taking ...?
What form of the medication is she taking?

Communicating with relatives by phone

Listening **1** Look at this list of things nurses say and do on the telephone. Which two are not recommended? Discuss.

		1	2
1	Say the name of the ward/department.	☐	☐
2	Say your name.	☐	☐
3	Offer to help.	☐	☐
4	Correct the caller's English.	☐	☐
5	Ask the caller to repeat something.	☐	☐
6	Put the caller on hold.	☐	☐
7	Apologise if there is a lot of noise in the background.	☐	☐
8	Talk to another person at the same time.	☐	☐

2 ▶ **36** Listen to two telephone conversations and tick ✓ the actions in 1 for each nurse.

Speaking **3** Work in small groups. Why is conversation 1 in 2 a bad example of how to communicate with people on the phone? Why is conversation 2 a good example? Make two lists.

In conversation 1, the nurse is stressed.
In conversation 2, the nurse is polite.

Language

Will

| We use **will** + infinitive to talk about the future. | *I'll just **check** he is awake.* |
| | *__Will__ he **be** out of surgery at eleven? Yes, he **will**./No, he **won't**.* |

---

4 Complete this conversation with *will* and the verbs in the box.

arrive	be	check	not come	take	transfer	wait

Nurse: Patients' Ward 2, Nurse Willard speaking. How may I help you?

Caller: Yes, hello, I'd like to speak to my husband in room 255, please. I want to tell him that I (1) _____ at the hospital very soon. But I (2) _____ by car today. I (3) _____ the bus, so I (4) _____ probably _____ late.

Nurse: Sorry about the noise here. Could you repeat the room number?

Caller: Room 255.

Nurse: Room 255. No problem. I (5) _____ just _____ he's awake and then I (6) _____ you. The medication we're giving him makes him a bit tired. Can I just put you on hold?

Caller: Sure, I (7) _____ .

Listening **5** ▶ 💿 **37** Listen to the first part of a telephone conversation between a nurse and a patient's relative and answer these questions. Write the answer or choose the correct words in *italics*.

1 What is the name of the hospital?
G_____ C_____ H_____
2 Which ward does the man call?
Emergency Room / Orthopaedics Ward
3 Why is the man's sister in the hospital?
She is giving birth. / She had an accident.
4 What is the patient's surname?
West_____

Speaking **6** ▶ 💿 **38** Put the second part of the conversation in 5 in the correct order. Then listen and check your answers.

Nurse: ☐ Do you have something to write with?
Caller: ☐ Thanks very much. I appreciate it. Bye.
Nurse: ☐ It's too early to tell. You'll need to speak to her doctor.
Caller: ☐ Thanks. I'll be there as soon as I can.
Caller: ☑2 Oh my goodness! Do you know if she's OK?
Nurse: ☐ Right. I'll inform your sister's doctor that you're coming.
Caller: ☐ Yes, go ahead.
Nurse: ☐ I'm afraid I can't give you any more information. You'll need to speak to her doctor when she's out of surgery. Would you like to come and wait at the hospital?
Caller: ☐ Are you sure? I really need to know if she's OK.
Nurse: ☑1 Ah, I see now. Your sister arrived at the ER this morning. She's in surgery at the moment.
Nurse: ☐ It's 22 Kennedy Road. There's a visitors' car park.
Caller: ☐ Yes, I think I'll do that. What's the address?
Nurse: ☐ Goodbye.

7 Read the conversation in 6 and underline examples of *will*.

Pronunciation **8** Read this information. Then draw the links between the words in the sentences.

> In English we often link words together when we are talking.
> consonant → vowel: Could I speak to ...?
> consonant → word beginning with /h/: I'll tell her doctor.

How can I help you?
How can I help you?

1 I see you're worried about her.
2 She's in surgery at the moment.
3 I'll help her when she's out of surgery.
4 I will inform her doctor that you're here.

9 Work in pairs. Take turns to read the conversation in 6. Link the words as you speak.

Speaking **10** Work in pairs. Practise a conversation between a nurse and someone asking about a relative in hospital. Include all the recommended elements in 1. Then swap roles and repeat the activity.

The hospital team

- move and handle patients
- communicate with team members by phone
- order supplies
- give simple safety instructions

Moving and handling patients

Speaking **1** Work in small groups. Discuss these questions.

1 When do nurses need to move patients? Make a list.
when the patient changes departments
2 What do nurses need to think about when they move a patient? Make a list.
the patient's weight

Vocabulary **2** Work in pairs. Label these pieces of equipment for moving and handling patients with the words in the box.

| banana board hand blocks hoist monkey pole rope ladder slide sheet |

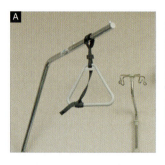

A
_____

B
_____

C
_____

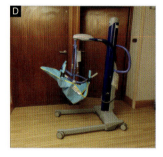

D
_____

E
_____

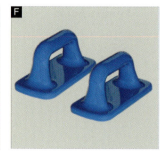

F
_____

Listening **3** 🔊 **39** Listen to three conversations. Which piece of equipment in 2 do the nurses use for each patient?

1 _____ 2 _____ 3 _____

4 Listen again and complete these sentences with the words in the box.

| pull up roll over sitting slide onto swing over |

1 She can _____ herself _____ to a _____ position.
2 Now _____ your legs _____ the side of the bed.
3 You can _____ the chair.
4 We're going to _____ you _____ onto your left side.

Language

The future: *be going to, will*		
Nurses use **be going to** + infinitive to explain an intention or a procedure (to the patient) before they do it.	First I'**m going to roll** you onto your side. Are you **going to get** a wheelchair?
Nurses use **will** for decisions made at the moment of speaking, for an offer (of help) or for predictions.	I'**ll go** and find a wheelchair. We'**ll help** you up now. She'**ll need** some help to get out of bed.

5 Complete this conversation between two nurses, Simin (S) and Phil (P), and a patient, Abdel (A), with the correct form of *be going to* or *will* and the verbs in brackets.

S: Hello, Abdel. Phil and I (1) _____ (help) you into a wheelchair so you can go and sit in the TV room. What do you think? (2) _____ (you / be able) to use the monkey pole?

A: I think so.

S: Good. And then Phil (3) _____ (help) you into the wheelchair.

A: This is great. I really want to see the football.

P: I (4) _____ (go) and find a wheelchair, Simin.

S: OK. Abdel, I (5) _____ (just / loosen) the sheets on your bed first. Now, can you pull yourself up? Hold onto the handle with both hands. Good, good, well done.

P: Wait a minute. I (6) _____ (bring) the wheelchair closer to make it easier for you. That's better. Now hold onto me and I (7) _____ (help) you into the wheelchair. There we go. How's that now, Abdel?

A: Great, thanks.

6 Work in groups of three. Practise the conversation in 5.

Reading **7** Read this training brochure and put the stages in the correct order. Then look at the conversation in 5 again and find examples for some of these stages.

> ### Moving and handling procedure
>
> ☐ Encourage the patient to co-operate.
> ☐ Adjust the height of the bed and/or loosen bed linen if necessary.
> ☐ Give clear instructions to the patient at each stage.
> ☐1 Explain what you are going to do and the reason for the move.
> ☐ Check if the patient is comfortable after the move.
> ☐ Explain your actions as you are performing them.
> ☐ Check that the patient agrees.
> ☐ Check the patient's level of independence.

Speaking **8** Work in groups of three. Student A, you are a patient. Students B and C, you are nurses. Read situation 1 below and think which piece(s) of equipment you need to move the patient. Roleplay the scenario, using the expressions and stages in 4 and 7 to help you. Then swap roles and do the same for situations 2 and 3.

1 Help a patient who is too weak to move from their bed to a wheelchair to go for a CT scan.

2 Turn a patient over and move them up their bed so that they are more comfortable.

3 Help an overweight patient onto their feet to go for a short walk.

Communicating with team members by phone

Speaking **1** Work in pairs. Answer these questions.

1 Why do nurses need to communicate with other medical staff by phone?
They need to book a porter to transfer patients to a different department or room.

2 What other ways are there to communicate with members of the team?

Listening **2** ▶ 🎧 40 Three nurses call to ask for porters to transfer their patients. Listen and complete the patient information.

 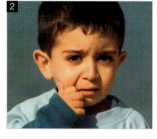 

Name: Tony Montana
ID N°: 811956
Patient room _____ →
Occupational Therapy

Name: Ali Murad
ID N°: _____
Paediatrics →
Radiology

Name: Karina Abramowicz
ID N°: 783359
Patient room 210 →
_____

3 Complete this telephone conversation with the words and phrases in the box.

accompany   ask for   double five   ID number
medical notes   porter   spell   transfer

Susie: Hello, Porter's Office, Susie speaking. How can I help you?
Davy: Yes, good afternoon, Susie. This is <u>Staff Nurse Davy Morris in ER</u>. I'm calling to (1) _____ a(n) (2) _____ to (3) _____ <u>Sylvia Tyler</u> to the <u>Orthopaedics Department</u>, please.
Susie: Could you give me the name of the patient again, please? And their (4) _____?
Davy: Yes, it's <u>Ms Sylvia Tyler, ID number 5521146</u>. Would you like me to (5) _____ that for you?
Susie: I think it's OK. Can you just repeat the ID number for me?
Davy: Yes, it's (6) _____ <u>two double one four six</u>.
Susie: OK, thanks. And who will (7) _____ the patient?
Davy: I will.
Susie: OK. Finally, can you confirm that all the patient's medical documents are ready?
Davy: Yes, we have the (8) _____, drug chart and all the nursing documentation.
Susie: Great, we'll send you a porter right away.
Davy: Thank you very much for your help. Goodbye.

Speaking **4** Work in pairs. Practise calling a porter to transfer one of the patients in 2. Use the conversation in 3 to help you. Change the underlined information. Then swap roles and repeat the activity.

Language

Past simple of *be*	
We use the **past simple of *be*** to talk about the past.	*The patient **was** in ER this morning.* *I **wasn't** in the handover meeting yesterday.* ***Was** his temperature up? Yes it **was**./No, it **wasn't**.*

5 Nurses Jenny and Pat are discussing the patients in 2 and 3. Write four short conversations about these patients using the past simple of *be*. You can invent some information. Then ask a partner to check your use of the past simple of *be*.

Jenny: Tony Montana was in the Emergency Department. Where is he now?
Pat: He wasn't in his room. I think he's in Occupational Therapy now.
Jenny: OK, thanks. I wasn't sure.

Listening 6 ▶ 🔊 **41** Listen to a telephone conversation between two colleagues, Sam and Glenda, and choose the correct words in *italics*.

1 Sam *leaves / takes* a message.
2 Glenda *leaves / takes* a message.

7 Read this training brochure about how to communicate effectively on the phone. Then listen again and tick ✓ stages 1–7 as you hear them.

> **Effective telephone communication between hospital staff**
>
> 1 ☐ Answer the phone – give your name, position and ward/department.
> 2 ☐ Offer to take a message.
> 3 ☐ Take the caller's number.
> 4 ☐ Read back the message.
> 5 ☐ Ask for confirmation.
> 6 ☐ Ask for clarification of details if necessary.
> 7 ☐ End the call.

8 Listen again and complete this telephone message.

> *(1) _____ to call (2) _____ in Pathology about Ms Shapiro's*
> *(3) _____ ; ext. (4) _____*

9 Look at the audio script for track 41 on page 78 and underline expressions for the different stages in 7.

Speaking 10 Work in pairs. Practise taking telephone messages. Use the information on the first telephone message card and roleplay the conversation with your partner. Then swap roles and do the same for the second card.

Caller: *Nurse Salih* Ext.: *44239* Message for: *Eddy Bull* Dept: *Radiology* About (patient name): *Rosie Hill* Message: *book appointment for X-ray on 3rd Dec, in afternoon*

Caller: *Sister Carter* Ext.: *23350* Message for: *Karine Jagger* Dept: *Summer Ward* About (patient name): *Ms Sandy Boyce* Message: *check patient details*

Ordering supplies

1 In a hospital supply room, items are often colour coded. Work in pairs. Look at illustrations A–L and put the items in the correct category.

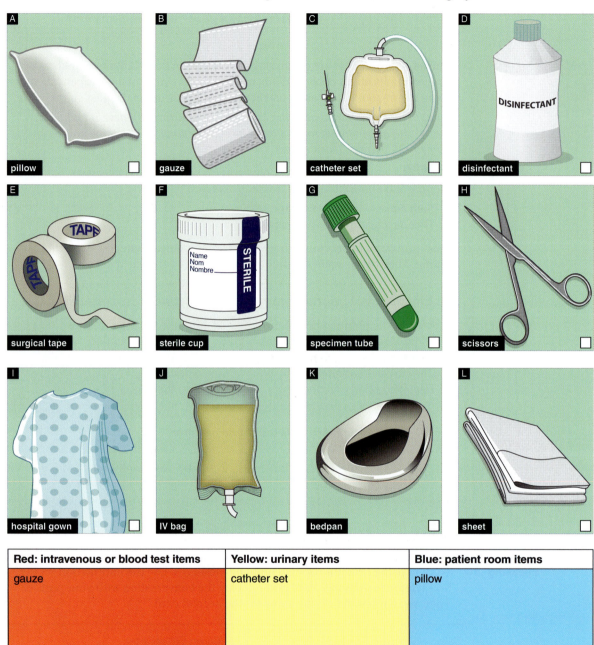

A	B	C	D
pillow ☐	gauze ☐	catheter set ☐	disinfectant ☐
E	F	G	H
surgical tape ☐	sterile cup ☐	specimen tube ☐	scissors ☐
I	J	K	L
hospital gown ☐	IV bag ☐	bedpan ☐	sheet ☐

Red: intravenous or blood test items	Yellow: urinary items	Blue: patient room items
gauze	catheter set	pillow

Listening **2** ▶ 🖭 42 Staff Nurses Cynthia and Louis are checking the inventory and ordering supplies. Listen to their conversation and tick ✓ the items in 1 that you hear.

3 Listen again and answer these questions.

1 For which rooms does Louis order supplies? For which floor?
2 What does Louis do to complete the order?
3 What did the hospital do a lot of this week?

Language

Any, enough	
We use **any** in negative sentences and questions with countable and uncountable nouns.	I can't find **any** pillows. Do we have **any** gauze?
Enough means 'as many or as much as is needed or wanted'. We can use it with countable and uncountable nouns.	Do we have **enough** surgical tape? Do we have **enough** sterile cups? Is/Are there **enough**? No, there isn't/aren't **enough**.
Remember: we use **much** and **many** when we ask questions with countable and uncountable nouns.	How **much** disinfectant is there? How **many** towels have we got?

4 Complete these sentences and questions with *much*, *many*, *any* and *enough*.

1 'Do we have _____ gowns?' 'Yes we do, but we don't have _____ .
How _____ do we need?'

2 How _____ blood do I need to take?

3 How _____ gauze do we need? Do we have _____ for the rest of the week?

4 'Are there _____ sterile cups in the storage room?' 'I think so.' 'How _____ are there?'

5 'Do we have _____ disinfectant in the OR?' 'No, we don't have _____ .'
'How _____ do we have?'

6 How _____ surgical tape do I put on this bandage? Is this _____?

Vocabulary **5** Match answers a–f to questions 1–6 in 4.

a) Just one specimen tube. ___

b) Yes. About three centimetres is enough. ___

c) There are about five boxes of 50. ___

d) No, we need to order 30 packs. ___

e) We need 28. ___

f) There are two bottles. ___

6 Match 1–4 to a–d to make phrases.

1 a box   a) of disinfectant
2 a pack   b) of gauze
3 a roll   c) of bandages
4 a bottle   d) of tape

Speaking **7** Work in pairs. Student A, look at the information on this page. Student B, look at the information on page 71. Follow the instructions.

Student A

1 You are a nurse and you need to order supplies. Phone Student B and order the items on your list.

We need:
* gauze (100 rolls)
* surgical tape (50 rolls)
* bandages (4 boxes)
* scissors (150)
* disinfectant (60 bottles)
* syringes (5 boxes of 50)
* specimen tubes (80)
* hospital gowns (45)

A: Hello, this is Nurse ... at ... Hospital.
I'm calling to order some supplies.
B: No problem. What do you need?
A: We need ...

2 Swap roles. Listen to Student B ordering supplies and write the items you hear.

Giving simple safety instructions

Vocabulary   **1**   Match the words in the box to these definitions. Then label the illustration with the words in the box.

> apron   disposable gloves   eye protection   mask   sharps box

1   This protects your mouth and nose. _____
2   This protects your clothes. You tie it around your waist. _____
3   This container makes it easy and safe to dispose of needles. _____
4   You wear these to protect your hands from the patient's blood and body fluids. _____
5   This helps protect your eyes. _____

a) _____
b) _____
c) _____
d) _____
e) _____

> sharps = sharp objects

Language

Past simple: regular verbs

To form the **past simple** of most **regular verbs**, we add -ed to the verb.	show – show**ed** clean – clean**ed**
Be careful of spelling changes: • verbs that end in -e: add -d. • verbs that end in consonant + -y: drop the -y and add -ied. • verbs that end in one vowel + one consonant: double the consonant and add -ed.	arriv**e** – arriv**ed** carry carr**ied** dr**op** – drop**ped**
We use the **past simple** to talk about actions and situations that started and finished in the past.	She **disinfected** the wound.

2   Look at the title of this article. Say what you think sharps injuries are. Then complete the article with the correct past simple form of the verbs in brackets.

Eliminating sharps injuries in the OR: a hospital tells its success story

Many years ago a team at Wilfred Johnson Hospital (1) _____ (organise) a project to reduce the number of sharps injuries. The OR supervisor, the hospital safety officer and a general physician (2) _____ (participate) in the project. They first (3) _____ (review) the information about injuries from the year before. This (4) _____ (show) that there were too many injuries with sharps, so the team (5) _____ (decide) to write new 'sharps safety rules' to explain the importance of safety. The new policy (6) _____ (include) clear directions for the staff who (7) _____ (use) sharps. The hospital (8) _____ (purchase) large boxes and put them in each OR. The team also (9) _____ (create) a new 'sharps zone', where staff members (10) _____ (pass) needles and knives on trays. After six months the number of sharps injuries (11) _____ (decrease). In 2008 the staff only (12) _____ (report) six sharps injuries. In 2009 the number (13) _____ (continue) to go down – to only three injuries!

Pronunciation

The endings of regular verbs in the past simple sound different.

3 🔊 43 Listen and repeat.

1 /d/: ordered, tied, changed
2 /t/: worked, fixed, stopped
3 /ɪd/: disinfected, protected, needed

4 🔊 44 Write the verbs in 2 in the correct group. Then listen and check your answers.

/d/	/t/	/ɪd/

Language

Expressing obligation: *always/never* + *if* clause

We use **always** or **never** + **if** clause to talk about an obligation.	**Always** wear gloves **if** you do a blood test. **Always** wear a mask **if** the patient has tuberculosis. **If** you use other materials, **never** put them in the sharps box.

5 Read this conversation between Sarah (S), a senior nurse, and Anja (A), a student nurse, and choose the correct words in *italics*.

S: If you give an injection, (1) *always / never* throw away the needle in the sharps box here.
A: What about the cap?
S: (2) *Always / Never* recap the needle. Just drop it in the box.
A: Why?
S: So you don't injure yourself with the needle. And we have a special place where we throw away the sharps boxes. If you want to throw away other materials like gauze or surgical tape, (3) *always / never* put them in the sharps box. Sharps boxes are very expensive and we have a special waste room in the hospital where we throw them away.
A: OK, I understand.
S: And if you take blood, (4) *always / never* use disposable gloves.
A: That's also part of the Universal Precautions Policy, right?
S: Yes. For your safety and your patient's. And in the OR, if you pass sharps like needles and knives, (5) *always / never* use your hands. (6) *Always / Never* use a tray.
A: OK. I can do all of that.

Speaking

6 Work in pairs. Practise the conversation in 5. Then swap roles and repeat the activity.

8

Recovery and assessing the elderly

- care for a patient in the recovery room
- remove sutures
- talk about old age
- assess an elderly care home resident

Caring for a patient in the recovery room

Listening

1 When a patient wakes up in the recovery room, a nurse usually asks them some questions. Complete the missing words in these questions.

1 ☐ Are you in any p_____?
2 ☐ Can you br_____ well?
3 ☐ What's your n_____?
4 ☐ Can you h_____ me?
5 ☐ Do you k_____ where you are?
6 ☐ Can you o_____ your eyes?
7 ☐ Do you f_____ nauseous?

2 ▶ 🎧 45 Listen to a conversation between a nurse and a patient and tick ✓ the questions from 1 you hear.

3 Listen again and answer these questions.

1 How often does the nurse take the patient's vital signs?
2 Does the nurse give the patient an oxygen mask?
3 Is the patient nauseous?
4 Is she cold?
5 What does the nurse give the patient?

> vital signs: pulse, temperature, blood pressure, respiration rate

Vocabulary

4 How does the nurse in 2 ask the patient about her pain? Put the words in the correct order to make the question. Then listen again and check your answer.

ten being the worst pain, / one being no pain at all, / what number is your pain right now / on a scale from one to ten, / ?

5 Work in pairs. Repeat the question in 4 five times with your partner.

Reading **6** When a patient is in recovery, a nurse has to take certain actions. Read these notes and put the actions in the correct order.

> ✳ ☐ *Check the patient's airway is open and clear.*
> ✳ ☐ *Compare the patient's vital signs with the anaesthesiologist's report.*
> ✳ ☐ *Check the identity of the patient.*
> ✳ ☐ *Listen to the anaesthesiologist give their report.*
> ✳ ☐ *Introduce yourself.*
> ✳ ☐ *Take the patient's vital signs every 15 minutes.*

Language

Past simple: irregular verbs

Irregular verbs do not form the past simple with *-ed*.	come – came give – gave tell – told
We use the past simple with **ago** to say when something happened.	The doctor left **ten minutes ago**.
To form the negative of both regular and irregular verbs, we use **didn't** + **infinitive**.	He **didn't speak** to the nurse. He **didn't eat** his dinner.
We form questions with **did**. The word order in questions changes: **did** + **subject** + **infinitive**.	**Did** you **write** the report? When **did** she **wake up**?

7 Write the past simple form of these verbs.

1 come   _____
2 wake up _____
3 bring   _____
4 leave   _____
5 tell   _____
6 go   _____

7 have   _____
8 give   _____
9 speak   _____
10 say   _____
11 drink   _____
12 eat   _____

8 Make these sentences negative.

1 He ate some of his dinner.
2 He drank a little water.
3 He had problems during the procedure.
4 We brought him to the recovery room.

9 Put the words in 1–7 in the correct order to make questions. Then answer the questions using the words in brackets. Write full answers.

1 when / Mr Wendall / surgery / did / come out / of / ? (five hours ago)
2 when / leave / the doctor / did / ? (a minute ago)
3 check / his vital signs / did / the nurse / ? (yes)
4 well / did / the surgery / go / ? (yes)
5 pain medication / give / did / him / the nurse / ? (yes)
6 speak / the nurse / to / did / the patient / ? (yes)
7 the patient / drink / what / did / ? (a little water)

Speaking **10** Work in pairs. Student A, you are a nurse. Student B, you are a member of a patient's family. Talk about his/her recovery. Use the sentences in 8 and 9 to help you.

Removing sutures

Language

Sequencers

We use *first*, *second*, *third*, *then* and *finally* to give instructions. We often use a comma after them.	**First,** wash your hands completely. **Second,** lift up the suture. **Third,** with the other hand, cut the suture. **Then,** check the wound is healed. **Finally,** clean and disinfect the wound.

Reading

1 Complete this text with *first*, *second*, *third*, *then* and *finally*.

Removing sutures

Before removing sutures, it is important to follow these directions.

When removing sutures, put on an **apron**. If you have long hair, be sure it is **tied back** securely. (1) _____, explain to the patient that you are going to remove their **sutures** (the patient will probably use the word *stitches*). (2) _____, ask the patient if he or she is comfortable. The patient may ask if it will hurt. Reassure the patient that removing sutures doesn't hurt. (3) _____, wash and dry your hands. Then prepare some gauze, **cleansing solution** and a **stitch cutter** on a **sterile tray**. (4) _____, put your hand inside a **sterile waste bag** and use it like a glove to remove the bandage from the sutures. Turn the sterile bag inside out so that the bandage is now inside the bag. Put on **sterile gloves**. (5) _____, look at each suture and check for inflammation around them.

2 Match the words in **bold** in 1 to illustrations A–H.

A
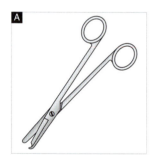

B
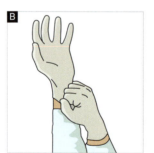

C

D
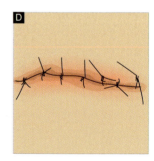

E

F
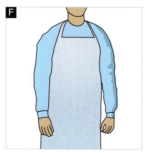

G

H

3 Read the text in 1 again. Are these sentences *true* (T) or *false* (F)? Correct the false sentences.

  1 Patients prefer the word *sutures* to *stitches*. (T / F)
  2 It always hurts when you remove stitches. (T / F)
  3 You should use a sterile bag like a glove to remove the bandage. (T / F)
  4 You should put on gloves after you remove the bandage. (T / F)
  5 You should check for inflammation after you remove the sutures. (T / F)

Vocabulary   **4** Read this conversation between a nurse and a patient and match the words in **bold** (1–8) to words with a similar meaning (a–h).

A: Mr Liber, it's time to (1) **remove** your (2) **stitches**.
B: Will this hurt?
A: You may just feel a (3) **pull**. Are you sitting comfortably?
B: Yes.
A: First, I'm just going to clean your wound. There. It looks good. The cut
    (4) **healed** nicely – no signs of infection.
B: That's good news.
A: Now I'll just (5) **cut** the suture near the knot, like this. With these (6) **scissors**
    I'll just pull out the stitch. How was that?
B: Fine – no problem.
A: Great. Now I'll just clean the wound again … and put some tape on your skin.
    Be sure not to (7) **take off** the tape.
B: OK. Can I take a bath?
A: It's better to shower for the first week to let it (8) **get better**.
B: OK, thanks.

a) stich cutter ____   e) take out ____
b) heal ____   f) snip ____
c) joined up ____   g) sutures ____
d) pull off ____   h) tug ____

Language

'Softener': *just*	
Nurses often use the word ***just*** before a verb to help reduce a patient's stress.	We'll ***just*** run a few tests. I'm ***just*** going to clean the wound with disinfectant.

5 Look at the conversation in 4 again and underline all the examples of *just*.

6 Rewrite these sentences using *just*. Then practise saying them to a partner.

  1 I'll lift up the suture.
  2 I'm going to cut the stitches with these scissors.
  3 I'll check to see there are no signs of infection.
  4 I'll leave these stitches in for three more days to let the wound heal.
  5 I'm going to put a new bandage on the wound.

Speaking   **7** Work in pairs. Practise the conversation in 4. Then swap roles and repeat the activity.

8 Work in pairs. Practise describing the procedure for removing sutures to your partner, a student nurse. Use the text in 1 and sequencing words. Then swap roles and repeat the activity.

First, put on an apron. Second, tie your hair back …

Talking about old age

Reading **1** Work in pairs. Discuss these questions.

1 When do you think old age begins?
2 Do you think a 75-year-old feels old?
3 How old would you like to live to?
4 Think about older people you know. What makes them happy?

2 Read this survey and answer the questions.

Growing old in the USA: a survey

In 2009 we asked 3,000 Americans about growing old. There were some interesting results.

When does old age begin?

There were different answers, depending on age and gender. Women generally said a person becomes old at 70 but men put the number at 66. Most 19-year-olds believed old age begins at 60.

Are you old?

Certainly not! Only 21 percent of respondents aged 65–74 and 35 percent of those aged 75+ said they feel old.

What age would you like to live to?

In 2002 most people wanted to live until the age of 92. In 2009 the majority said 89 years old. One in five would like to live into their nineties, and eight percent say they would like to live to 100 years or older.

Are older people happy?

The answer to the question was yes. 34 percent of respondents aged 30–49 said old people were 'very happy' and only 14 percent believed they were 'not too happy'. 28 percent of 75-year-olds said they were 'happy', and only 12 percent thought they were 'not too happy'. Finally, what makes the older generation happy? The answer is good health, good friends and financial security – the same things that make younger generations happy.

Where should old people live?

1 When do most young people say old age begins?
2 What percentage of 75-year-olds feel old?
3 What age would most people like to live to?
4 What makes older people happy?

Speaking **3** Work in pairs. Discuss these questions. Then compare your ideas with another pair.

1 How are elderly people cared for in your country? In the family?
   In specialised care homes? In their own home with community assistance?
2 Why do some people think a care home is the best place for the elderly?

Vocabulary **4** Look at illustrations A–J and write facility (*F*) or activity (*A*) in the boxes. Then say which facilities and activities you think an ideal care home should have.

A garden ☐	
B TV room ☐	
C exercise programme ☐	
D day trip ☐	
E computer room ☐	
F laundry room ☐	
G aromatherapy treatment ☐	
H dining room ☐	
I nature walk ☐	
J library ☐	

Listening **5** ▶ 🎧 46 Listen to a conversation between a nurse and Edwin, a new care home resident, and write down the facilities and activities from 4 you hear.

6 Listen again and answer these questions.
1 What are Edwin's hobbies and likes?
2 Why doesn't Edwin like TV?
3 How many children does Edwin have?
4 Why is the internet so important for Edwin?

Language

Offering advice and making suggestions
We can use these expressions to give advice or make suggestions:

why don't you/we + infinitive	**Why don't you send** your son an email?
you/we could + infinitive	**We could go** for a walk on the beach.
it's a good idea to + infinitive	**It's a good idea to speak** to your doctor about your pain medication.

7 Complete these conversations with expressions from the Language box and the correct form of the verbs in brackets.

1 A: I often feel lonely and miss my family.
   B: _____ (put up) some photos of your family in your room?

2 A: I like sport but I have to be careful because of my arthritis.
   B: Well, _____ (join) the exercise class with Sally.

3 A: My father seems sad. I'm worried about him.
   B: _____ (speak) to the senior nurse to check on his progress.

4 A: I never see my grandchildren but I really want to keep in touch.
   B: _____ (send) them an email or join them on Facebook?

5 A: My mother wants to wash her own clothes. Is that possible?
   B: We have a laundry room here. _____ (call) the manager and ask her about it first.

Assessing an elderly care home resident

Vocabulary **1** Work in pairs. Label photos A–F with the aids in the box.

| commode | dentures | glasses | grabber | hearing aid | walking frame |

A 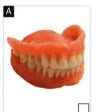 ☐

B  ☐

C  ☐

D  ☐

E  ☐

F 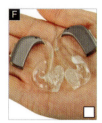 ☐

_____ _____ _____ _____ _____ _____

2 Match 1–6 to a–f to make sentences about the aids in 1. Then match the sentences to the photos in 1.

1 Patients use this when they
2 Patients wear these when they lose
3 Patients wear these in order
4 Patients use this to pick
5 Patients wear this to
6 Patients use this to help

a) hear better.
b) up objects they cannot reach.
c) are not able to walk to the toilet.
d) them walk around more easily.
e) to see better.
f) their natural teeth.

Listening **3** 🔊 **47** Listen to the first part of a conversation between a nurse and Dipak Gyawali, a new care home resident, and choose the correct words in *italics* in this assessment form.

Assessment form

THE BEECHES
CARE HOME

Personal
- I would like to be called (1) *Mr Gyawali / Dipak*.
- I'm happy when (2) *I see my family / I'm by myself*.
- (3) *Impolite or unfriendly people / Noisy places* make me angry.
- My favourite foods are (4) *Spanish and French / Italian and Indian*.
- Foods I dislike are bananas and (5) *eggs / fish*.
- I (6) *wear / don't wear* dentures.

4 🔊 **48** Listen to the second part of the conversation in 4 and complete the rest of the assessment form.

Hobbies and interests
- My hobbies and interests are sports – (1) _____, and (2) _____ – and music – (3) _____ and (4) _____ Indian music.
- I watch (5) _____ on TV. I listen to (6) _____ on the radio. I (7) _____ magazines.

Mobility
- I use a(n) (8) _____ and a(n) (9) _____ to move around.
- I (10) _____ to use a commode.
- I find it difficult to bend, so I use a(n) (11) _____ to pick things up.

Communication
- I (12) _____ hearing problems.
- I (13) _____ eyesight problems, so I wear (14) _____ .

5 Compare your answers in 3 and 4 with the rest of the class.

Writing **6** Work in small groups. Why do you think it is important for care home nurses to ask questions like the ones in the conversation in 3 and 4? Make a list.

Language **7** Complete these questions from the conversation in 3 and 4 with the words in the box.

| are   can   do   how   what (x3)   when   who |

1 _____ would you like us to call you?
2 _____ do you feel?
3 _____ do you enjoy doing?
4 _____ are the children in the photo?
5 _____ makes you angry?
6 _____ you have any favourite foods?
7 _____ there any foods you don't like?
8 _____ you walk to the bathroom by yourself?
9 _____ did you last see your family?

8 Work in pairs. Ask and answer the questions in 7. Use the information in 3 and 4 to help you.

Speaking **9** Work in pairs. Student A, you are a new care home resident. Read case study 1 and complete this assessment form. Invent some of the information. Student B, you are a nurse. Interview Student A. Then swap roles and repeat the activity for case study 2.

Assessment form

Personal
• I would like to be called _____ .
• I'm happy when _____ .
• _____ make(s) me angry.
• My favourite foods are _____ .
• Foods I dislike are _____ .
• I *wear* / *don't wear* dentures.

THE BEECHES
CARE HOME

Hobbies and interests
• My hobbies and interests are _____ .
• I *watch* / *don't watch* _____ (on) TV. I *listen* / *don't listen* to _____ (on) the radio. I *read* / *don't read* magazines.

Mobility
• I *use* / *don't use* a(n) _____ to move around.
• I *find* / *don't find* it difficult to bend (, so I use a(n) _____ to pick things up).
• I *use* / *don't use* a commode.

Communication
• I *have* / *don't have* hearing problems (, so I wear _____).
• I *have* / *don't have* eyesight problems (, so I wear _____).

Case study 1
Ms Sandy McDonald is 80 years old. She has hearing problems. She has difficulty walking and needs to use a commode at night. She wears dentures.

Case study 2
Mr Derek Simpson is 92. He wears dentures, has poor hearing and wears glasses. He finds it difficult to walk without a walking frame. He needs to use a commode.

Partner files

1 Meeting colleagues

Reading a nursing schedule

Speaking exercise 5 page 7

Student B

Look at this hospital facilities schedule. Take the role of patient or visitor and ask Student A questions to complete the information.

	Midland Town Hospital Hospital Facilities
Visiting hours	_____ _____
Car park	Monday to Friday: 7.30 a.m. – 9.00 p.m.
Bank	Weekdays: 10.00 a.m. – 12 noon and 1.00 p.m. – 3.00 p.m.
Restaurant	Monday to Friday: 7.30 a.m. – 5.30 p.m. Saturday and Sunday: _____
Coffee shop	Monday to Friday: 8.30 a.m. – 6.30 p.m. Saturday and Sunday: _____
Gift shop	Monday, Wednesday, Thursday: _____ Tuesday and Friday: 10.00 a.m. – 2.00 p.m. and 5.00 a.m. – 8 p.m. Saturday and Sunday: 10.00 a.m. – 5.00 p.m.
Newsstand	Monday to Friday: _____ Saturday and Sunday: 12.00 noon – 8.00 p.m.
Patient mealtimes	Breakfast: 7.30 a.m. Dinner: _____ Tea: 5.00 p.m. Beverages: _____

What are the visiting hours?
What are the opening hours of the bank?
What time does the car park open/close?
When is breakfast?

Meeting patients and their visitors

Speaking exercise 5 page 8

Student A

1 You are a nurse. Practise meeting your patient. Introduce yourself and ask questions about the family in Student B's picture.

Student B

You are a patient. Answer Student A's questions.
A: Is this your family?
B: Yes. This is my son and this is his wife.

2 Swap roles and repeat the activity.

2 Nursing assessment

Checking patient details

Speaking exercise 6 page 13

Student B

1 You are a nurse and Student A is a patient. Ask Student A questions to complete this patient record.

> **Patient details**
>
> **GH**
>
> Name: _____
> Gender: _____ male _____
> DOB: _____
> Country of origin: _____
> Telephone number: _____
> GP: _____
> Email: _____
> Address: _____
> Next of kin: _____
> Relationship to patient: _____

2 Swap roles. You are the patient and Student A is a nurse. This is your patient record. Answer Student A's questions.

> **Patient details**
>
> **GH**
>
> Name: Chandrika Bandaranaike
> Gender: female
> DOB: 03.04.1955
> Country of origin: Sri Lanka
> Telephone number: 011-91-097-70445779
> GP: Nimal Ariyawathi
> Email: maakd@glide.net.in
> Address: 4 Kodambakkam High Road, Nungambakkam, Ahmedabad 380006
> Next of kin: Ranjit Bandaranaike
> Relationship to patient: husband

Describing symptoms

Speaking exercise 8 page 15

Student B

1 Ask Student A about his/her symptoms and tick ✓ the symptoms he/she has.

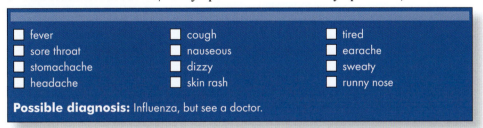

> ☐ fever   ☐ cough   ☐ tired
> ☐ sore throat ☐ nauseous   ☐ earache
> ☐ stomachache ☐ dizzy   ☐ sweaty
> ☐ headache   ☐ skin rash ☐ runny nose
>
> **Possible diagnosis:** Influenza, but see a doctor.

Hello, how do you feel today? Do you have a temperature? Do you have a sore throat?

2 Swap roles. You are ill and these are your symptoms.
   You
   - have a very bad cough.
   - have a bad sore throat.
   - are dizzy.
   - have a runny nose.

   Answer Student A's questions, explaining your symptoms. Student A will give you a possible diagnosis.

5 The body and movement

The body: torso and head

Speaking exercise 4 page 39

Student B

You are on the telephone. Student A needs to fill in the Range of Motion (ROM) exercise record for a patient, Mr Ahmad. Answer his/her questions.

Movement	Repetitions	Comments	Nurse initials
Shoulder rotations	Repeat ten times.	Mr Ahmad should sit on the bed. Left shoulder only.	
Hip bends	Repeat five times.	Do this on the bed. Hold his head and neck in your hands.	
Head lifts	Hold for five seconds, then put down. Repeat three times.	This is difficult for him because of the pain in his neck.	
Chest lifts	Hold for three seconds, then put down. Repeat five times.	Give him a ball to hold near his face. He pushes the ball up.	

Documenting ROM exercises

Student B

Speaking exercise 8 page 43

Listen to Student A. Then swap roles. Read Joe's flow sheet for 8th March and explain to Student A which exercises the patient can and can't do.

Flow sheet – Range of motion exercises

GCH General Central Hospital

Patient: Joe Felicie   **Room N°:** 214   **Date:** 08.03.2012

Movement	Time		Comments
	12.00	17.00	
R shoulder flexion		✓	WNL
R shoulder rotation		✓	WNL
R hip abduction		✓	WNL
R hip extension		✓	WNL
L shoulder flexion		✓	WNL with some pain
L shoulder extension			limited to 100°
L hip abduction			limited to 90°
L hip extension			limited to 45°
L knee extension			limited to 25°
Nurse's initials:			

Joe can bend his right shoulder normally. He can …

6 Medication

Side effects; assisting patients with medication

Speaking exercise 9 page 49

Student B

Ask Student A questions to fill in the rest of Doris' medication record.

Personal medication record		Patient: *Doris MacDonald*			**GCH** *General Central Hospital*
Medication	**Reason for use**	**Form**	**Route**	**How much & when?**	**Side effects**
Azopt	glaucoma	drops	_____	one drop, three times a day	_____ _____
insulin	diabetes	_____	stomach	_____ _____	itching, mild pain, redness or swelling at the injection site
Metamucil	constipation	syrup	_____	15 mg, three times a day	_____
Tamiflu	cold	capsules	_____	75 mg, two a day for five days	_____
multivitamins	general health	_____	mouth	_____	nausea

Why is Doris taking ...?
What form of the medication is she taking?

7 The hospital team

Ordering supplies

Speaking exercise 7 page 57

Student B

1   Listen to Student A ordering supplies and write the items you hear.

2   Swap roles. You are a nurse and you need to order supplies. Phone Student A and order the items on your list.

We need:
* *sterile cups (10 packs of 100)*
* *IV bags (200)*
* *sheets (15)*
* *blankets (15)*
* *pillows (30)*
* *towels (50, small size)*
* *bedpans (40)*
* *catheter sets (20)*

A: *Hello, this is Nurse ... at ... Hospital. I'm calling to order some supplies.*
B: *No problem. What do you need?*
A: *We need ...*

Unit 1 Meeting colleagues

▶ 🎧 02

1 A: Hello, I'm Staff Nurse Gillian Campbell.
  B: Hi, I'm Amy Bower. I'm a healthcare assistant for Ward C.
  A: Nice to meet you, Amy.

2 A: Excuse me, are you Ward Sister Margaret Jenkins?
  B: Yes, I am.
  A: Pleased to meet you. I'm Charge Nurse Paul Gallagher.
  B: Good to meet you, Paul.

3 A: Hi. My name's Paul.
  B: Hello, Paul. I'm David. So, where are you from, Paul?
  A: I'm from Dublin. I'm the new charge nurse. What do you do on the ward?
  B: I'm a student.

▶ 🎧 03

[T = Tyler; K = Karen]
T: Hi, Karen, it's Tyler Baker.
K: Oh, hello, how are you?
T: Good, thanks, Karen. Listen, can you give me my schedule for this week, please?
K: Sure. Is the afternoon shift OK for you?
T: I have exams in the mornings, so the afternoon shifts are perfect, yeah.
K: OK, so you start on Tuesday at 16.45 and finish at 23.00. On Wednesday, you start at 15.30 and finish at 22.15; and it's the same on Thursday.
T: That's good for me.
K: Are you free on Friday, Tyler? I need a staff nurse for St Peter's Care Home in Hillsworth.
T: I'm not free on Friday, no. But Saturday ... I can work on Saturday.
K: OK. Can you do a morning shift at the Amazon Hospital?
T: No problem. What time is the shift?
K: 6 a.m. till 2 p.m.

▶ 🎧 04

[C = Mrs Coxen; A = Anja]
1 C: Yes?
  A: Good evening, can I come in?
  C: Yes, of course.
  A: Hello. It's Mrs Coxen, isn't it?
  C: Yes, hello.
  A: My name's Anja. I'm taking care of you this evening.

[K = Katya; W = Mr Williams]
2 K: Good morning, Mr Williams. Can I help you?
  W: Well, yeah, but where's the other nurse?
  K: Ellie works on the night shift. I'm Katya and I'm taking care of you.
  W: OK, right, good. Look, I need ...

[M = Max; SA = Susie Arnold]
3 M: Good afternoon. Mrs Arnold?
  SA: Susie; please call me Susie. Good afternoon.
  M: Hi, Susie, I'm Max. Sorry to disturb you. I'm looking after you. How are you today?

[D = Denny; K = Kendra]
4 D: Hello, it's Kendra, isn't it?
  K: Yes.
  D: Hello, Kendra. My name's Denny. I'm looking after you. Is that OK?
  K: Yes.
  D: And who's this?
  K: It's my teddy. His name's Mr Willis.
  D: Well, hello, Mr Willis. And how are you today?
  K: I have a poorly arm.
  D: A poorly arm? Can I look?

▶ 🎧 05

D: Hello, it's Kendra, isn't it?
K: Yes.
D: Hello, Kendra. My name's Denny. I'm looking after you. Is that OK?
K: Yes.
D: And who's this?
K: It's my teddy. His name's Mr Willis.
D: Well, hello, Mr Willis. And how are you today?
K: I have a poorly arm.
D: A poorly arm? Can I look?

▶ 🎧 06

A X-ray machine
B CT scanner
C MRI scanner
D ECG machine

▶ 🎧 07

[N = Nurse; AK = Amira Khan; DS = Dorothy Simpson; EK = Emilia Kadinska]

1 N: Good afternoon, Ms Khan. Are you ready for your ECG?
  AK: I suppose so.
  N: Can I just look at your identity bracelet? Thank you. What is your full name, please?
  AK: Amira Khan. That's K-H-A-N.
  N: And your date of birth?
  AK: 1st February 1956.
  N: Thank you. Can I swipe the code on your bracelet? All done, thanks.

2 N: Mrs Simpson? Mrs Simpson? Sorry, Mrs Simpson. How are you?
  DS: OK, dear, thank you.
  N: Mrs Simpson, it's time for your CT scan.
  DS: Already?
  N: Yes. Can I look at your identity bracelet first? Thanks. What's your full name?
  DS: Dorothy Simpson.
  N: How do you spell 'Simpson', please?
  DS: Oh ... ah ... S-I-M-P-S-O-N.
  N: And what's your date of birth?
  DS: 22nd June 1932.
  N: 1932. Thank you, Mrs Simpson.

3
N: Emilia? Hello. Are you ready for your X-ray?
EK: Sure.
N: Can I see your ID bracelet, please?
EK: Again?
N: Afraid so. It's important we have the right patient.
EK: Right. My name's Emilia Kadinska. That's K-A-D-I-N-S-K-A. And my date of birth is 16th April 1998.
N: Thanks, Emilia. And can I swipe the code? That's great. All correct.

▶ 🔊 08

[K = Kelly; J = Jake]
K: Hello. How are you this morning, Jake?
J: A bit tired.
K: It's time for your X-ray now. Are you ready?
J: Oh, OK.
K: Can I just see your identity bracelet first, please? Thanks. What's your full name?
J: Jake Peterson.
K: Your date of birth?
J: 18th January 1982.
K: 18th January 1982. OK. Can I swipe the code on your bracelet, please? That's it, thanks.

▶ 🔊 09

[K = Kelly; J = Jake; C = Claire]
K: Can you walk to the X-ray Department, do you think?
J: Is there a wheelchair or a walking stick, maybe? I'm a bit weak this morning.
K: There's a wheelchair.
J: I prefer that, thanks.
K: Of course. Let me help you. There you are. Are you warm enough?
J: I'm a bit cold, actually.
K: Let me give you a blanket. Is that better?
J: Thanks.
K: Here we are at Radiology. Morning, Claire.
C: Kelly, hi.
K: Claire, this is Jake Peterson. He has an appointment for an X-ray at 10.30.
C: Good morning, Jake. I'm Claire. I'm taking care of you today and ...

Unit 2 Nursing assessment

▶ 🔊 10

[A = Adviser; H = Mrs Herriot]
1
A: Good morning, Health-Connect, how can I help you?
H: Yes, hello. I need a doctor for my little boy, please. He's got this rash and I'm really worried about him.
A: I understand your concern. I just need to take his details, and our practice nurse will call you back.
H: Oh, OK, sure.
A: Can you give me your son's full name?
H: Yes, it's James Herriot.
A: Can you spell the family name for me, please?
H: H-E-R-R-I-O-T.
A: Is the last letter *P* as in *Peter*?
H: No, *T* as in *Thomas*.
A: And your name, please?
H: Anna Herriot.
A: What is your relationship to the patient?
H: I'm his mum.
A: OK, thanks. And can you give me your phone number, please?
H: 775-932-8053.
A: Thank you, Mrs Herriot. One of our practice nurses will call you back in the next 30 minutes.

[A = Nurse Ayali; K = Mr Kamil]
2
A: Mr Kamil, good morning. Please take a seat. I'll be with you in a moment. Sorry about that. Now, what can I do for you?
K: Morning, Nurse Ayali. I'm here for my blood test.
A: That's right. I just need to check your patient record first if that's OK. Please confirm your full name and date of birth for me.
K: Amir Kamil. Kamil – K-A-M-I-L. I was born on 9th January 1973.
A: Thank you. And where do you live? I have 32 Avenue Mohammed-V.
K: No, I don't live there any more. My new address is 81 Avenue Mahmoud Diouri.
A: Can you spell Diouri, please?
K: Yes, it's D-I-O-U-R-I.
A: D-I-O-U-R-I. And do you have an email address we can use?
K: akamil@teleco.com – that's A-K-A-M-I-L at T-E-L-E-C-O dot com.
A: OK, thanks. I'll pass these details on to the receptionist.

▶ 🔊 11

A I have a runny nose.
B I have a headache.
C I have stomachache.
D I have a cough.
E I have a fever.
F I feel itchy.
G I have a skin rash.
H I have a sore throat.
I I have earache.
J I have swollen glands.
K I feel tired.
L I feel sweaty.
M I feel dizzy.
N I feel nauseous.

▶ 🔊 12

[C = Chelsea; M = Mother; N = Nurse]
1
C: My head hurts, Mummy.
M: I know, sweetheart. The nurse is going to look at you. Do you still feel sick?
C: No.
N: Can I just feel your neck, Chelsea? That's right. Yes, it's swollen, isn't it? Is she still nauseous?
M: No, she isn't.
N: OK, it looks like she has ...

[N = Nurse; M = Milly; F = Father]
2
N: Hello, what's your name?
M: Milly.
N: That's a pretty name. Now, Milly, can I have a look at your ears? You have a little rash there and your glands are swollen, I see. Does this hurt?
M: Yes, it does.
N: And a fever. You're very hot, aren't you? Does she have any other symptoms?
F: She has a runny nose.
N: Sore throat?
F: Yeah, a little ...

[N = Nurse; I = Isabelle; M = Mother]

3 N: How are you today, Isabelle?
I: I have a bad sore throat.
N: Do you have a cough?
I: Yes, and ... and spots.
N: Spots? Really? Can you show me?
I: Yes. I've got them here and here, look.
N: Oh, yes, a skin rash.
I: My best friend, Kelly, she has spots, too.
N: Does she? Ms Quinn, does Isabelle have any other symptoms?
M: She's got a bit of a fever and cold symptoms – runny nose, you know.
N: Right. OK then, Isabelle; let's have another look at that rash.

▶ 🔊 13

[N = Nurse; A = Alessandro]
N: Is this your first blood test, Alessandro?
A: Yes, it is, and I really don't like blood.
N: OK, well, let's go step by step. Please roll up your sleeve for me. Let me disinfect your arm first. Now let me tie the tourniquet round your arm. OK, now you'll feel a small pin prick.
A: Oh! That's tight.
N: It won't take long. Now turn your head to the window. What can you see?
A: I see a school. There are lots of children, a teacher, I think ...
N: Uh-huh, yes? Now I just need a minute to change the specimen tube.
A: Uh-oh. I feel really dizzy.
N: That's OK. Now hold this cotton ball to your arm. Press hard for a minute and bend your arm. Yes, that's right. Take a deep breath and close your eyes. Good.
A: I don't like this.
N: Keep breathing. It's done now. Now for the plaster ... and I'll send this to the lab.
A: I don't feel so good.
N: Here's some juice; that will help your dizziness.
A: Thanks.
N: Just relax. How do you feel now?
A: Much better. I feel much better ...

▶ 🔊 14

1 If you feel faint, let me know.
2 If you feel weak, tell me.
3 If you feel nauseous, let me know.
4 If you feel hot, tell me.

Unit 3 The patient ward

▶ 🔊 15

1 oral
2 tympanic
3 electronic
4 thermometer
5 temperature
6 disposable

▶ 🔊 16

A: Good morning, Fred. How did you sleep last night?
B: OK, thanks. Not bad.
A: Is it OK to take your temperature?
B: Sure, no problem.
A: Can you open your mouth for me, please? And can you just put this under your tongue? That's it. Now could you close your mouth and hold for a minute? Good, I think that's done. Can I just take out the thermometer?

Thanks. Let's have a look.
B: Is it normal?
A: Your temperature is 36.9 degrees this morning. It's fine.
B: What are you doing now?
A: I'm just recording it on your temperature chart.

▶ 🔊 17

clean supply room
conference room
nurses' lounge
nurses' station
patient room
physicians' area
soiled utility room
visitors' toilet

▶ 🔊 18

[S = Steve; K = Kelly]
S: Do you like your new job then, Kelly?
K: I do, yes. The people are all really friendly. It's a good team.
S: What about the patient ward?
K: It's a bit small and we have to share some of the facilities with other patient wards.
S: Oh. Aren't there any patient rooms? There are more than 20 in our ward.
K: Of course there are patient rooms, Steve! But there isn't a conference room, for example; and there aren't any visitors' toilets either.
S: Strange. There are two conference rooms in our ward but only one visitors' toilet. Is there a nurses' station?
K: Yes there are two small ones. What about where you work?
S: There is one big nurses' station and two small ones. What about a nurses' lounge?
K: There isn't one in our department, no.
S: Shame, our nurses' lounge is great. There's a TV, a microwave, free tea and coffee, DVDs ...

▶ 🔊 19

[SW = Shelly Wagner; A = Mrs Azziza; J = Jerome; P = Mr Patel]

1 SW: Hello, Mrs Azziza, how can I help you?
A: Nurse, oh, thank you for coming. I really, really need to go to the toilet. Thanks for coming.
SW: OK, no problem. Let me help you out of bed. There we go. Here's your walking frame. Do you need any help with ...

2 SW: Yes, Jerome, this is Shelly, what can I do to help?
J: Is that Nurse Wagner?
SW: Yes, it is. Can I help you?
J: Yes, Nurse, please. I'm very thirsty and there's no more water in the jug.
SW: Right, OK. I'll bring you more water in a few minutes. Is that OK?
J: In a few minutes? Oh, OK.
SW: Can I help you with anything else, Jerome?
J: Er, yes, can you turn off the TV? I want to try and sleep.
SW: I'm coming in a few minutes, OK?

3 SW: Mr Patel, you rang. How can I help you?
P: I'm really sorry to disturb you, Nurse ...
SW: You're not disturbing me. What can I do for you?
P: I have a terrible pain in my leg. It won't stop and I can't sleep.
SW: It's OK, I'm here. Please try to relax. I'm calling the doctor now and we're going to help you. The doctor will give you some more pain medication. Just try to breathe ...

🔘 20

[H = Nurse Henshaw; F = Mr Fredericks]
H: Mr Fredericks, it's Nurse Henshaw. How can I help you?
F: I can't … I can't breathe!
H: OK, I'm going to help you. Let's put your bed up first. That's better. Now I want to give you some oxygen. Let's put the mask on. Is that better?
F: No … no … I feel hot. I'm … I'm really worried. What's happening?
H: It's OK, I'm here. Keep your mask on. Try not to talk. I'm calling the doctor now. OK, please try to relax. You're in good hands. Look at me and breathe with me. Good. You can slow your breathing down now. That's it. How are you feeling now?
F: A little better, but my chest feels so tight.
H: Keep breathing with me, it's OK. Good. The doctor is here. We're taking care of you.

Unit 4 Food and measurements

🔘 21

1 A: Here's the menu, Mr Robertson. What would you like today?
  B: I'd like a piece of quiche, some mashed potatoes and an orange, please.
  A: Would you like a drink?
  B: Please, yes. Can I have some coffee?
2 A: My order's ready.
  B: OK. Can I just check it first?
  A: Yeah, sure.
  B: Spaghetti bolognaise and a turkey sandwich? I'm sorry, Michela; you can only have one main course. What would you prefer, spaghetti bolognaise or a sandwich?
  A: Um… a sandwich, please.
  B: OK. One turkey sandwich. What about a dessert and a drink?
  A: An apple, please and … and some cola. Thanks.

🔘 22

1 a hundred and sixty
2 a hundred and nineteen
3 one thousand and fifty
4 one thousand, two hundred
5 eighteen
6 one point two five

🔘 23

1 A: And how many calories are there in a glass of orange juice?
  B: About 168, I think.
  A: How many glasses of orange juice can I order?
  B: Just one for now, I think. How much apple purée do you want?
  A: Just a little.
2 A: How much milk can I have, Nurse Webster?
  B: You're on a 2,000-calorie diet.
  A: That's right, yes.
  B: So you can drink a couple of glasses a day if you like.
3 A: Nurse Chueng, just a little question.
  B: Yes?
  A: Can I order a glass of milk and a cup of coffee? I'm not sure how many calories there are in a cup of coffee.
  B: There are no calories in black coffee and only 90 calories if you take fat-free milk.

4 A: Nora, sorry, can you tell me how many calories Mrs Kelly is allowed?
  B: She's on a low-calorie diet for the next few days, so that's 1,200 a day.
  A: OK, thanks. Just checking.

🔘 24

1 kilo
2 calorie
3 litre
4 kilojoule
5 kilogram
6 millilitre

🔘 25

[N = Nurse; C = Cherif; L = Lydia]

1 N: So, what would you like to order for your lunch today, Cherif?
  C: I have problems swallowing. What do you suggest?
  N: Why not have a cheese omelette? It's easy to eat.
  C: Yes, but I don't really like omelettes. What's the vegetable lasagne made of?
  N: It's a dish with tomatoes and peppers with pasta and a cheese sauce. It smells good, anyway.
  C: OK, I'll have that.
  N: Would you like to order anything else?
  C: Yes, I'd like some orange juice and some fruit salad for dessert, please.
  N: Great, all done. Give me your menu card and I'll hand it in for you.

2 L: Sorry, Nurse, can you help me with my menu order? My daughter is going to bring in my reading glasses; I can't read the menu without them.
  N: Yes, of course, Lydia. Let's have a look.
  L: I'm a vegetarian, so what can I have today?
  N: Well, how about some lasagne or the tomato and mozzarella salad?
  L: Is it vegetarian, the lasagne?
  N: Yes.
  L: OK. And am I allowed to eat the cherry tart?
  N: I'm afraid you're on a restricted diet for the next few days, Lydia. There's yoghurt on the menu today. Would you like that?
  L: I would like some honey or sugar with it. Is that possible?
  N: It's served with honey, yes. And would you like a starter? There's orange juice.
  L: No, it's OK; that will be too much.

🔘 26

[PM = Paula Minelli; T = Mrs Taylor]
PM: Mrs Taylor, hello. Would you like some help with your meal today?
T: Yes, please. My hands are shaking and I don't want to spill anything, if possible.
PM: Let me just wash my hands and find an apron. OK, ready. Would you like a straw for your orange juice?
T: Please.
PM: There you go. It's OK, take your time, Mrs Taylor.
T: I'm sorry; I'm just not very hungry.
PM: You're doing well. How about some more orange juice?
T: I think that's all I can drink, thanks.
PM: You're having the chicken and vegetables – it smells really good. How much can you eat today?
T: A little. Maybe half of it.

PM: That's good. Would you like some help with your vegetables? I can cut them up for you.

T: Thanks, but you know, I don't think I really want any.

PM: Can you just try a little?

T: OK, just a little bit.

PM: That's good.

T: I really can't eat any more.

PM: Just one more potato?

Unit 5 The body and movement

🔊 27

[N = Nurse; D = Mr Dubois]

N: OK, Mr Dubois, it's important to do these exercises every day to help you.

D: All right; you're the boss. Can I stay in bed?

N: Yes, sir. It's important that you are comfortable. Let's start with your feet. Now keep your heels on the bed and push your toes to the end of the bed.

D: Like this?

N: Yes, that's right. Push your left foot, then your right foot. Good. Now try and rotate your foot in a circle.

D: That's easy. No problem.

N: That's good because this exercise is really important. Can we try your legs now?

D: Oh that will hurt.

N: Well, you are taking pain medication, so it might not hurt too much.

D: OK …

N: Now lift your right leg. Bend your knee just a little. Now move your leg to the side of the bed. That's right. Let's do that again ten times.

D: Ten!

N: Yes, ten. Let's count together. One, two, three, four … You're doing really well.

🔊 28

[N = Nurse; P = Patrick; H = Hugo; J = Juan]

1 N: Patrick, back already from physio? How are the exercises going?

P: It's slow, Nurse, but you know …

N: Well, what's your long-term goal?

P: For the moment, I just want to climb the stairs by myself. It's very simple, really. My wife usually helps me. It's difficult in our house.

N: Uh huh?

P: I sleep in the living room but the bathroom is upstairs, so …

2 N: OK, Hugo, so one of your goals is to be able to eat by yourself.

H: Yeah, sure. After the accident this is still difficult for me.

N: OK. What do you want to do today?

H: My shoulder is really painful. I can't do the shoulder exercises today.

N: That's fine. What can you do?

H: I think the wrist exercises are OK.

N: Good. Well, let's start with those. We'll stop if it hurts.

3 J: I think my arms are getting stronger. I can already put on some of my clothes by myself.

N: That's great news, Juan. Well, for today our goal is three sets of ten on each arm. Can you do that?

J: OK with me.

N: Can you do this exercise three times a day?

J: Yes, I think so.

🔊 29

1 What do you want to do today?
2 Can you do this exercise three times a day?
3 What can you do?
4 Can you do that?

🔊 30

[N = Nurse; T = Thelma]

N: OK, Thelma, let's see what you can do today. Our goal is three sets of ten on each leg. What do you think?

T: I'll try. It's more difficult on the left leg.

N: OK, we'll try the right leg first, then. Ready?

T: OK, yes.

N: Move your leg out to the side as far as you can. That's right.

T: That's OK?

N: You're doing very well, Thelma. And then back. Now let's repeat that. Good, good. And once more. Out to the side … and back. Again … and relax. Very good. A little rest?

T: I'm OK, thanks.

N: Now for the left leg. Are you ready? Tell me if it hurts, OK?

T: OK.

N: So, let's try. Move your leg out to the side. That's it. Just a little higher … and back. That's better, well done!

T: Yeah, that's really difficult.

N: Yes, but it's much better than yesterday. Much better. Let's try again. Out to the side … a little higher … and back.

T: I'm sorry, it's too painful.

N: Let's stop now. I think it's a good idea.

🔊 31

[C = Nurse Carter; SN = senior nurse]

C: Joe is doing much better today.

SN: That's good to hear.

C: Yeah, he's just done his nine o'clock exercise session. He has normal movement in his right shoulder now – he performed both rotation and flexion exercises very well.

SN: What about the hip exercises?

C: He can do the abduction and the extension exercises but he still has a lot of pain in his right hip. And as for exercises for the left shoulder, he can only do the shoulder flexion to 100 degrees and he can't do the shoulder extension exercises at all for the moment. I'm writing up the flow sheet now. Do you need any other information?

Unit 6 Medication

🔊 32

1 A: Good morning, Katy. How are you feeling?

B: A little tired.

A: Do you still have the nausea?

B: Yes, I do.

A: OK. I can give you something to control the nausea if you want.

B: Oh yes, please.

A: Do you have enough water? Good. Please take two tablets now. You can swallow them with water.

2 A: I think I'll have to give my husband his drops. Ted won't be able to do it himself.

B: Yes, I think you're right.

A: What is the dosage?

B: That's three drops into his right ear now, Mrs Mathews, and then again just before he goes to bed.

A: OK, that's easy enough. Thanks for your help.
B: You're welcome.

3 A: What are these for, Nurse? I've forgotten.
B: The capsules are for your heart problems, Mrs Fox, for the angina.
A: That's right. I forget, I'm sorry.
B: We all forget from time to time. Now let me explain the dosage. You take 25 mg now with a glass of water. The second one at lunchtime, then again at around 7 p.m. And the last one when you go to bed.
A: Oh that's a lot to remember.
B: Would you like me to write the times down for you?
A: Would you, dear? That's very kind of you.

4 A: We're going to give Ali Haddad his antihistamine injection now. Would you like to come and observe?
B: Can I practise giving him the injection?
A: As a student you can only watch, I'm afraid.
B: I understand.
A: His next injection will be in the evening, at 22.00.
B: OK. Actually, I saw Ali earlier; his skin rash is a lot better, isn't it?

33

1 A: Mr Johnson is to get 60 mg of Lasix. We have 20 mg tablets on hand. How many tablets will you give him?
B: I divide 60 mg by 20, which equals three. So that's three tablets.

2 A: If you infuse 250 ml over two hours by IV, what is your flow rate per hour?
B: Um, OK ... 250 divided by two hours, which equals 125 ml per hour, I think?
A: Yeah, that's right.

3 A: Billy needs 1.5 mg per kilogram of Solumedrol and he weighs 28 kg. How many milligrams will you give him?
B: If I do 28 kg multiplied by 1.5, which equals 42 mg, then I give 42 mg. Is that right?
A: Yeah, that's right. Good.

34

Today we're talking about side effects. We'll look at the most common drugs first. As you know, some patients suffer side effects and others don't. And not all patients suffer the same side effects either. Let's consider ibuprofen, for example, a very common pain medication. Some people may suffer dizziness and others might feel nauseous. It's also possible to have diarrhoea, vomiting, even headaches with this type of pain medication. Injecting drugs intravenously may cause swelling at the injection site for some patients. Stomachaches are a side effect of some anti-allergy drugs, as well as loss of appetite and constipation. Patients who take Valium may experience drowsiness; others may get a skin rash. Tremors are another side effect of this drug.

35

[N = Nurse; D = Doris]
N: Right, Doris, let's have a look at your medication record together, shall we? Can you show me all your medication first?
D: Here you are – here's the drops for my eyes, my insulin and the Metamucil.
N: OK, now write down the name of each medication in the chart.
D: OK. First for my eyes – Azopt. That's A-Z-O-P-T. Then my insulin for my diabetes ... then Metamucil. Let's see how you spell that ... M-E-T-A-M-U-C-I-L.
N: What about over-the-counter medication?
D: I'm taking Tamiflu at the moment. I have a bad cold.

N: Yes, I can tell. Do you take any vitamins?
D: Just multivitamins. Shall I write these down, too?
N: Yes, write down everything. You're suffering from constipation at the moment, Doris?
D: Yes, I think it's a side effect of the insulin. My GP prescribed me Metamucil.
N: That's good, but I don't think constipation is a side effect of insulin.
D: Oh.
N: Well, I think that's everything.

36

1 A: Oh shoot, this is just not my day today! Yes ... yes, hello?
B: Uh ... hi. Is this patient department?
A: What?
B: Is this patient department?
A: What? Oh, you mean the patients' ward. Well, it depends. We've got three of them.
B: I call for my husband. He in room 204.
A: Oh yeah, hang on ... yeah. Room two zero what? Hang on a second. Can you just give me a second? I'm on the phone. Yeah, what room number was that again?
B: Room 204. Mr Fang.

2 A: Patients' Ward 2, Nurse Willard speaking. How may I help you?
B: Yes, hello, I speak to my husband in room 255, please.
A: Sorry about the noise here. Could you repeat that?
B: Room 255.
A: Room 255. No problem. I'll just check he's awake and then I'll transfer you. The medication we're giving him makes him a bit tired. Can I just put you on hold?
B: No problem. I wait.

37

A: Hello, General Central Hospital, Orthopaedics Ward. Nurse Wilson. How can I help you?
B: Yes, hi. I'm calling to get some information about my sister. She was in a car accident and I'm really worried about her. I really need to know if she's OK.
A: Can I have your sister's name, please?
B: Uh ... Jeanne. Jeanne Westberry.
A: Jeanne ... sorry ... Westdury? D-U-R-Y?
B: No, -berry. B-E-double R-Y.
A: B as in Beatrice, E-R-R-Y?
B: Yes, that's right.
A: Let me just check.

38

A: Ah, I see now. Your sister arrived at the ER this morning. She's in surgery at the moment.
B: Oh my goodness! Do you know if she's OK?
A: It's too early to tell. You'll need to speak to her doctor.
B: Are you sure? I really need to know if she's OK.
A: I'm afraid I can't give you any more information. You'll need to speak to her doctor when she's out of surgery. Would you like to come and wait at the hospital?
B: Yes, I think I'll do that. What's the address?
A: Do you have something to write with?
B: Yes, go ahead.
A: It's 22 Kennedy Road. There's a visitors' car park.
B: Thanks. I'll be there as soon as I can.
A: Right. I'll inform your sister's doctor that you're coming.
B: Thanks very much. I appreciate it. Bye.
A: Goodbye.

Unit 7 The hospital team

▶ 💿 39

1 A: Dan, can you come and help me with Ms Marsh, please?

B: No problem.

A: She has a rope ladder, so she can pull herself up to a sitting position but she'll need some help to get out of bed.

B: Are we going to use a hoist?

A: No, I don't think we need a hoist. Ms Marsh only weighs about 45 kilos, poor thing.

B: Oh, OK.

2 A: Mr Baxter, we're going to help you into your chair. You'll be more comfortable for watching the TV. Carol is going to lower your bed first.

B: And what's that?

A: You've never seen one of these before? Great, isn't it? It's called a banana board. Now can you sit up first, please? That's it. Now swing your legs over the side of the bed. I'm going to put the banana board on your bed and – and now you can slide onto the chair. Careful now … slowly. There you are.

3 A: Kenny, are you ready? We're going to roll you over onto your left side.

B: Just a second – my leg. OK. I'm OK.

A: Are you sure? OK, so we'll roll you over. Good. I'm going to put this slide sheet on the bed and now we'll roll you over again onto your back.

▶ 💿 40

1 A: Hello, is that the Porter's Office?

B: Yes, it is. Can I help you?

A: Yes, please. This is Sister Marshall from Kelmann Ward, and I'd like a patient transferred to Occupational Therapy, please.

B: Certainly. Can you give me the name of the patient and the room number, please?

A: Yes, that's Room 211 and the patient's name is Tony Montana. Shall I spell that for you?

2 A: Yes, the Porter's Office, please.

B: Yes, you're through. How can we help you?

A: Good morning. This is Staff Nurse Ania Pershik in Paediatrics. I'm calling to ask for a porter to transfer one of my patients to Radiology for his scan.

B: No problem. Can you give me the patient's details, please?

A: Yes. It's Ali Murad, ID number 992163 …

3 A: Good evening, Porter's Office.

B: Yes, hello. I'd like a porter to transfer a patient of mine, please.

A: OK. Can I have some details, please?

B: Sure, the patient's name is Karina Abramowicz. She's in Room 210 and she needs to go to the Maternity Department. As quickly as possible, please.

A: OK. I just need to take a few more details first …

▶ 💿 41

[S = Sam; G = Glenda]

S: Good afternoon, East Ward. Staff Nurse Sam Turner speaking. Can I help you?

G: Hello, Sam. This is Glenda Davies from Pathology. Can I speak to Nurse Wright, please?

S: I'm sorry, she's on her lunch break at the moment. Can I take a message for her?

G: Yes, please. Can you ask her to call me back? I have Ms Shapiro's test results.

S: Yes, of course. What's your number?

G: It's extension 8391.

S: OK, so if I can just check the message: that's Nurse Wright to call Glenda … I'm sorry can you repeat your family name, please?

G: Davies. D-A-V-I-E-S.

S: Nurse Wright to call Glenda Davies in Pathology about Ms Shapiro's test results on extension 8391.

G: That's right. Thanks very much for your help. Goodbye.

S: Bye.

▶ 💿 42

[C = Cynthia; L = Louis]

C: Hi, Louis. Sorry I'm late. I was in the laboratory and I had to wait for some results. I'm here to help you with the inventory.

L: OK, Cynthia, you can use this scanner and I'll take this one. And you scan the items we need to order. For example, we need new hospital gowns and sheets for the patient rooms on the fourth floor. So you scan the code like this … and you enter the number we need. We need nine of each. To finish that order, press 'enter' on the scanner.

C: OK, I understand. I know we need to order some more bedpans. And we need a lot more gauze and surgical tape.

L: OK. We also did a lot of blood tests this week during the blood donation campaign, so we need some more specimen tubes and IV bags.

▶ 💿 43

1 ordered, tied, changed
2 worked, fixed, stopped
3 disinfected, protected, needed

▶ 💿 44

1 organised, reviewed, showed, used, continued
2 purchased, passed, decreased
3 participated, decided, included, created, reported

Unit 8 Recovery and assessing the elderly

▶ 💿 45

[N = Nurse; W = Mrs Wendall]

N: Mrs Wendall? Can you hear me?

W: Yes.

N: I'm your recovery room nurse. Your heart bypass surgery went well.

W: Good.

N: I'm going to take your vital signs every 15 minutes and check your oxygen levels. This mask will help that. Can you breathe well?

W: Yes. My chest hurts.

N: On a scale from one to ten, one being no pain at all, ten being the worst pain, what number is your pain right now?

W: I guess five.

N: OK. Do you feel nauseous?

W: No. But I feel cold.

N: Here's a blanket. How is that?

W: Better, thanks.

▶ 💿 46

[N = Nurse; E = Edwin]

N: It's Edwin, isn't it? When did you arrive?

E: Only a couple of days ago. I'm still getting used to the place. I really miss my own home – my garden and my neighbours, especially.

N: You know, there's a nice little garden here. We could go and sit out there tomorrow if you like.

E: Sounds like a nice idea. Why not?

N: What do you like doing? Do you have any hobbies?

E: I like nature and I read a lot. I saw the TV room yesterday but I don't really like TV any more – I have hearing problems and I don't have the patience to read the subtitles.

N: We organise nature walks, usually in the summer. We go for short walks along the beach, into the woods. We also organise day trips to historical sites. And if you like reading, we have a small library with novels and magazines. Why don't you go to the library this afternoon? It's open till 4 p.m.

E: I might do that, thanks. What about internet access? The manager said there was internet access.

N: Yes, there is. We have a small computer room. It's a good idea to reserve a time to use the computer. It's more and more popular with the residents. And what about your family? Where do they live?

E: My son and his wife are in Australia, and my daughter lives in Canada. So I keep in contact by email. The internet is very important to me.

N: I can imagine. Listen, it's about time for lunch. Why don't we go into the dining room? I want to introduce you to some of the others.

E: Sure. I was getting hungry.

▶ 💿 47

[N = Nurse; DG = Dipak Gyawali]

N: Good afternoon, Mr Gyawali, nice to meet you. My name's Anna. My team will be taking care of you during your stay at The Beeches.

DG: Nice to meet you, too.

N: Now, I'm just going to ask you some questions first so that we can get to know you better. Is that OK?

DG: Yes, of course.

N: First question: what would you like us to call you?

DG: I prefer people to call me Dipak if that's OK.

N: Yes, of course. It's your first day here, Dipak – how do you feel?

DG: A little sad.

N: Yes? Can you tell me why?

DG: I miss my own house, my garden. I like my independence, so you see, I'm … I'm sorry.

N: It's OK, I understand it's difficult for you at the moment. I hope we can make it easier for you. We're going to try, anyway. So, when do you feel happy?

DG: That's easy – when I spend time with my family.

N: And who are the children in the photo?

DG: My grandchildren, Sunita, and that's Razu.

N: Ah, they're beautiful! When did you last see your family?

DG: I visited them last month.

N: You can tell me more about them later. What makes you angry?

DG: What makes me angry? Well, I don't like people who are impolite or unfriendly.

N: OK. Now, your favourite foods. Do you have any favourite foods?

DG: I love Italian and Indian food, so curry, pasta, that kind of thing. And fruit – pineapple, mango …

N: Good. Are there any foods you don't like?

DG: Bananas – I'm not a fan – and eggs. I am allergic to eggs.

N: That's important for us to know, thank you. Do you wear dentures, by the way?

DG: Yes, I do, unfortunately. I hate them.

▶ 💿 48

[N = Nurse; DG = Dipak Gyawali]

N: Do you have any hobbies, Dipak?

DG: Yes, I like sports.

N: Oh, yes. What sports do you follow?

DG: I like tennis and cricket – and I usually watch the big games on TV.

N: When will the next big cricket match take place?

DG: In the summer.

N: OK, we'll have to remember that. Anything else you like doing?

DG: I like music, too – classical and traditional Indian music.

N: Do you watch TV, listen to the radio, read magazines or a newspaper?

DG: TV for the sports, and I listen to the news on the radio. I don't really read magazines though.

N: I see you use a walking stick in the home?

DG: Yes, and I used to use a walking frame to go to the shops, for example. I can't walk for a long time without it.

N: OK, that's noted. How about the rest of your mobility? Can you walk to the bathroom by yourself, for example, or do you need to use a commode?

DG: No, I don't need a commode but I do find it difficult to pick things up.

N: We can provide you with a grabber if you like. And finally, you don't wear a hearing aid, so … not hard of hearing. But do you need glasses?

DG: Yes, I'm short-sighted; I need them for watching TV.

Pearson Education Limited
Edinburgh Gate
Harlow
Essex CM20 2JE
England
and Associated Companies throughout the world.

www.pearsonelt.com

First published 2012

ISBN: 978-1-4082-6993-0

Set in ITC Cheltenham Book
Printed by Graficas Estella, Spain

Acknowledgements
The publishers and author would like to thank the following
people and institutions for their feedback and comments
during the development of the material:

Peggy Labat; France; Krystyna Key, Germany; Shobha
Nandagopal, Oman; Anke WinklerPrins, USA

The publishers would like to thank the following for their kind
permission to reproduce their photographs:

Alamy Images: Bubbles Photo Library 4tc, By Ian Miles-
Flashpoint Pictures 4bl, Catchlight Visual Services 16 (A),
itanistock 45 (Ali), 54 (2), Medical-on-line 52 (B), Sam
Edwards 32c, Science Photo Library 20 (A), UpperCut
Images 4tr; **Art Directors and TRIP Photo Library:**
Helene Rogers 10 (D), 20 (B), 52 (A), 52 (C), 52 (D), 66
(B); Corbis: moodboard 54 (3); **Courtesy of MEDesign Ltd
@ www.medesign.co.uk:** 52 (F); **DK Images:** Andy
Crawford 20 (C); **Fotolia.com:** Alexander Raths#31062925
35, dotweb.dk#21226728 66 (F), fred goldstein#453082 20
(D), Hakan Kızıltan #34370069 10 (B), Konstantin Shevtsov
#7726133 10 (A), lunamarina#25259948 54 (1), Natalia
Merzlyakova#28402383 66 (D), romarti#20140160 66 (E),
Tom McNemar#36364 66 (C), Yuri Arcurs #22472326
45 (Ted); **Getty Images:** Berhard Lang 21, Felbert +
Eickenberg 32l; **Pearson Education Ltd:** Jules Selmes 33
(A), 33 (B), Photodisc / Kevin Peterson 33 (C), 45 (Katy),
Photodisc / C Squared Studios 66 (A); **Photofusion
Picture Library:** John Birdsall 4tl; **Quintal Healthcare Ltd:**
52 (E); **Science Photo Library Ltd:** Dr. P. Marazzi 16 (B),
Mark Thomas 4br, PR. PH. Franceschini 16 (C);
Shutterstock.com: James Steidl 10 (C), sima 45
(Suzanna), Supri Suharjoto 32r

Cover images: *Front:* **Construction Photography:**
Buildpix l; **Getty Images:** David Trainor background, LWA /
Larry Williams c; **SuperStock:** Tetra Images

All other images © Pearson Education

Every effort has been made to trace the copyright holders
and we apologise in advance for any unintentional
omissions. We would be pleased to insert the appropriate
acknowledgement in any subsequent edition of this
publication.